New I
RIOTOUS I

This book is dedicated to my teent   *l. He was born in the middle of a great*   *:e his Howard ancestors, active in New I*   *...…vulutionary War, he has overcome many adversities and has pledged himself to "Live Free or Die!"*

A British cartoonist shows how New Englanders treated informers and tax collectors — "tar and feathers, and hot tea poured down the throat."

Cover Photos: ISBN 0-916787-12-5

Paintings of George Washington at his desk and Indians at the Tea Party, courtesy of the John Hancock Mutual Life Insurance Company, Boston: Pen and ink sketch of drummer from Dedham and fifer from Cambridge at Battle Of Bunker Hill, courtesy Leslie's Retreat Restaurant, Salem, MA; Two caricatures of Redcoats by Peter F. Copeland, "Uniforms of the American Revolution," Dover Publications, Inc., New York. Engraving - Boston Massacre, copied from Paul Revere's original engraving.

INTRODUCTION

Although American history was not one of my favorite subjects during my early school years, the teachers did make me aware of the suffering and sacrifice of our noted Colonial heroes. The cousins Adams, who spearheaded the Revolution, John Hancock, who exhausted his fortune helping to finance it, Paul Revere on his famous ride, and James Otis who made great speeches; all working in common cause to gain Independence for the Thirteen Colonies. I learned what they did during their finest moments, and what they said to stimulate Americans into rebellion, but I was never quite sure who they really were. Were they super-human, I often wondered, or just regular guys, determined not to let the British push them around? Was it just these leaders who stimulated New Englanders into war with the most powerful nation on earth, or were there other leaders, unsung heroes, who were willing to fight and die to gain freedom for themselves and for us? Over 225 years have passed since that first spark of rebellion ignited in New England, yet we know very little about those who gave us so much.

We have grown up in America with only good words to describe our Revolutionary War patriots, but when they were alive, none of them were treated with such awe and respect. Robert Treat Paine, for example, called John Adams *"a numbskull,"* and Adams called Paine *"conceited."* John Adams, who became second President of the United States, said that the great patriot-orator James Otis was *"foul-mouthed,"* and cousin Sam Adams referred to Otis as *"a very horney man."* A newspaper reporter described John Hancock as *"a milk-cow,"* and added, *"whether public spirit or vanity has been his governing spirit, is uncertain."* Paul Revere, who was disgraced with a court-martial during the war, was considered by some of his neighbors to be *"greedy"* and *"a poor artisan who copied everything he did from other artisans."* Sam Adams, noted *"Father of the Revolution,"* was called by his contemporaries *"a poor student, and a failure at everything he attempted in life."* Before becoming famous, Sam was a debtor, and almost went to jail for stealing public funds. Otis, who was called *"the mad dictator of Boston,"* thought John Adams was *"an intellectual snob,"* and Hancock was often called a snob, but not an intellectual one. Sam Adams was a slob in the way he dressed, and Revere was always out to make a buck, any way he could. He actually charged his mother when she borrowed a half-cup of sugar from him, and he sent a detailed bill to Massachusetts for his Midnight Ride, which can be seen today at the State Archives in Boston. Apparently Robert Treat Paine had the same vice, for John Adams writes in his diary that, *"Paine aims at so many things, but especially at getting cash."* Paine wrote that *"Adams is impudent, ill-bred and a conceited fellow,"* and so you have our great American heroes, all New Englanders, who obviously, at times, thought little of each other — but together, through seemingly insurmountable trials and tribulations, led this country into rebellion and the eventual parting with Mother England.

Another misconception about the Revolution is that most Americans were involved in fighting the British, when actually, just as many Americans joined the British to fight their fellow Americans, and an equal number remained neutral, taking neither side in the War. Some Revolutionary War historians mention that since America was made up of Englishmen and descendants of Englishmen, the Revolution was more like a civil war of Englishmen fighting Englishmen, which is far from the truth. A survey-census of the time shows that only 52% of the 3,930,000 people living in America were English born or of English descent during Revolutionary times, 15% were Blacks, and 95% of them were slaves, 10% were born in Ireland, 6% were German, 5% Scots, and the rest were Dutch, Poles, Italians, Spaniards, Frenchmen, Scandinavians, Jews, and native Indians — and this census included only the American Indians who lived within the Thirteen Colonies. Even the British army and navy fighting in America was made up of Germans, Austrians, Dutch, Irish, Welch, Scots, Americans, and Blacks — less than one-third of the British forces were English-born — so it certainly wasn't a war of Englishmen fighting Englishmen. It is true, however, that most military officers on both sides were English or descendants of Englishmen.

This little book was prepared not only to give you an insight into the true character of the heroes and villains active in the early stages of the American Revolution, but to introduce you to some of the characters who got little or no publicity then or now, yet played a vital part in the rebellion — and to provide information on some of the hilarity and hardships experienced by the average Yankee as he stuggled for freedom in enemy-controlled New England.

Bob Cahill

I
A MIDGET AMIDST GIANTS

George was a common first name in America before the Revolutionary War, for King George II and King George III were popular then, and the name George was of course popular after the war because of George Washington. George Robert Twelvetrees Hewes was born August 25, 1742. He was named after his father George, who was a tanner, glue-maker, chandler, soap-boiler and jack-of-all-trades in Boston Towne. He was given the second name of Robert for his uncle who was a blacksmith in Boston. The middle name of Twelvetrees was passed down to him from his mother, Abigail Sever Hewes, who had a lovable Great Uncle whose last name was Twelvetrees. Father George didn't like the name Twelvetrees, and since mothers didn't go to christenings in those days, he asked the minister of the church to shorten baby George's middle name on the baptismal record to *"Twelves."* Deacon Drowne, however, misunderstood, and spelled it *"Twells."* As sophisticated as the name sounds, the Hewes family of fourteen was poor and lived in near squalor on Water Street near the docks of North Boston. The kids growing up in the area, Ben Franklin and Paul Revere among them, were tough and water-wise, fondly referred to as *"water-rats"* by their adult counterparts. As a youth George Robert Twelves Hewes not only had to live down his name, with taunts from his peers and occasional fist fights on the piers, but his size as well. His father, who died when George was ten, stood 4-feet 6 inches tall, and his mother was no taller, but George didn't even reach their heights, growing to 4-feet 4 inches by age 17 and never gaining another inch.

At age 15, after spending a few months in school, a few more months as an apprentice shoemaker, and running away from both, he went fishing at the Grand Banks with his brothers — he had six of them. Then, he decided to join the army. England and France were at war, and the upper territories, Maine, Vermont and New Hampshire, were threatened by the Canadian French and Indians. The Massachusetts Militia had already been called out in the spring of '56, and a year later, 3,500 more volunteers were needed to march to Vermont. George and his pal John Gilbert enlisted, but before being accepted by the Muster Captain, who received two dollars for each new recruit, they had to be examined on Boston Common. When Captain James Cox came face-to-face with young Hewes, standing in the ranks at attention on his tip-toes, he merely commented, *"You're too short Hewes."* George was obliged to leave the Common. He immediately went to the nearest cobbler shop and purchased leather pads to build up the heels of his shoes, and then he stuffed paper and rags into the shoes until, he concluded, *"I was at least three inches taller."* He returned to the Common and walked directly to Captain Cox who was still reviewing recruits. Cox wasn't fooled. *"I never seed a man grow so tall so fast,"* he said loudly for the entertainment of the other militiamen. *"Why if my corn grow'd that fast, I'd be the wealthiest farmer in New England."* Embarrassed, George limped home.

"The young scamp," as John Hancock called him, then tried to join the crew of a privateer. She was moored at dockside and would sail to battle off Nova Scotia once her skipper had the needed complement of men. George was accepted and had his sea-bag stashed aboard, when four of his brothers, at their mother's insistence, stomped aboard like a press-gang and dragged George, yelling and screaming, from the privateer. The skipper was unhappy, as was George, but the privateer sailed without him. Four months later word was received at Boston that the privateer sank in a storm off Cape Breton and that all hands were lost at sea. George had been so angry at his mother that he moved out of the house at Water Street and into a nearby boarding house, but he thanked her when he heard what had happened to the privateer.

Little George had to go back to the only trade he knew besides fishing — shoe making. He was working at a cobbler shop at the head of Griffen's Wharf when the men came home from the French and Indian War with tales of adventure. One was George's cousin, Davy Orne, and another was his neighbor Paul Revere, both only a few years older than himself. Neighbors and friends flocked to the pub on nearby Hitchbourn wharf, owned by Revere's mother, to learn about their victory. Mrs. Revere was a Hitchbourn, one of *"a wild, unruly family."* She had married Apollos Rivoire, a French Huguenot, who had settled in Boston when he was 13 years old. He changed his name to Revere because Bostonians didn't pronounce Rivoire correctly. He worked as a gold and silversmith, just down the street from James Franklin's printshop, where brother Ben Franklin started his career as a printer's-devil and as a youth ran away from his dictating brother to Philadelphia. Also working nearby as an apprentice in the import-export business was Tom Hancock, John's uncle, who married Lydia Henchman, the fat but rich boss' daughter. When Tom Hancock died, he left his merchant shipping business, retail stores, and most of his money to young John. Apollos Revere, however, died leaving little to his wife and nine children, and the oldest boy, 19 year old Paul, just back from the war, took over the responsibility of supporting his brothers and sisters.

George remembered one story Paul Revere told at Hitchbourn's

Pub, for it suggested that there was a strong anti-British sentiment in New England as far back as the late 1750s. Most soldiers returning home from the French and Indian War concluded that the English displayed a snobbish superiority towards America's *"country bumpkins."* Davy Orne even sang a song that a British doctor named Shuckburh made up to go to the tune of an old English schoolboy melody titled *"Lucy Locket"*: *"Yankee Doodle went to town, riding on a pony, met an Injun in the hay and asked to be his croney. Yankee Doodle keep it up, Yankee Doodle Dandy, don't mind the feathers, eat them up, and with your gun be handy."* Revere didn't join in, for he had a terrible off-key singing voice, but he explained to his neighbors and friends that *"Yankee"* was what the British soldiers now called Americans, derived from an old Scots Gaelic word meaning *"hag-like,"* and *"Doodle"* meant *"a half wit."* A *"dandy"* was someone, usually of the upper class, who wore extravagant clothes. The American soldiers were well aware that the popular British ditty was a put-down of them. Paul had heard one British colonel call the boys from Boston *"a motley drunken bunch,"* but Paul explained to the crowd that *"us Yankees got even. At Ticonderoga, General Abercromby of the British Army asked us to clear the charges from our muskets by firing them. There was some fine firing for a spell, but you see, old Abercromby didn't tell us in what direction to fire in. Some of our men shot the British colonel through the head and kilt him. Must have been ten holes through the poor bugga, but nobody knowd who kilt him."* A few weeks later, Paul married Sarah Orne, Davy's sister, and took over his dad's silversmith shop.

One day a real *"Dandy,"* the *"tall, gaunt, but always eligantly dressed"* John Hancock came into the shoemaking shop to ask George Hewes to repair a boat-pump. Hancock seemed to take a liking to the little man, but George admitted that he was nervous in the presence of this *"vain, proud, aristocratic man,"* even though John was only five years his elder. Upon leaving the shop, Hancock asked George to visit him at his mansion on Boston Common that New Year's Day. Arriving at the front door of Hancock's splendid home on Beacon Hill, George was so nervous that he bowed to the butler. The butler ushered him into the kitchen, thinking he was a servant, but when George told him that he was John Hancock's guest that day, the butler brought him into the sitting room. *"Take a chair, lad,"* said John, as he welcomed George and gave him a glass of wine, recently smuggled into Boston from the Canary Islands. George had never had alcohol before, and it went to his head. *"We drank to our health and I gave a pretty speech,"* said George, *"then Mister Hancock put his hands in his breeches pocket and pulled out a crown-piece, which he placed in my hand."* John then shook George's hand and said, *"Come again next New Years,"* and the butler escorted Hewes out the door. Hancock often handed out coins to Bostonians who he considered poor or down-and-out, but he obviously didn't want to spend much time with people he considered *"riff-raff."* George, however, didn't seem to mind, and he always held *"Mister Hancock"* in high esteem.

Hancock was at the coronation of King George III in England in 1760, and the king gave him a gold snuffbox as a gift. The new king and John were both 22 years old at the time and very impressed with each other, but nothing like the impression that was to come. As Boston churchbells tolled the joyous news of a new king, a new Royal Governor of Massachusetts, Sir Francis Bernard, was appointed. Until he arrived in Boston, however, a local lad and legislative councilor, Thomas Hutchinson would be acting governor. Hutchinson, like Hancock, was a wealthy aristocrat and was also noted as a local historian. Seemingly *"old skin and bones Tommy"* was liked well enough by the people of Boston. However, when he was appointed Chief Justice of the Commonwealth as well, most local merchants were upset, for this gave him control of the judicial, legislative, and executive branches of government. *"I oppose that kind of power,"* shouted James Otis Jr. of Barnstable, leading attorney and orator of New England, *"which in former periods of English history, cost one king of England his head and another his throne."* It wasn't just Hutchinson's power or the taxes and restrictions imposed on America by Britain that infuriated Otis, but that his father had been promised the position of Chief Justice by the Crown. Sir Francis Bernard had passed him over to appoint Hutchinson. So angry was young Otis that he gave up his position as Advocate General of the Admiralty and represented 60 local merchants who petitioned the court against England's enforcement of the *"Writs of Assistance"* — a law allowing customs officials to break into any American's home or warehouse in search of supposedly smuggled goods. Actually, the *"Writs"* had been in effect for many years, and smuggling goods in and out of New England ports had become a way of life for the merchants. The new king and his ministry, however, replaced the old Boston tax collector, who, for a slight fee, often allowed vessels in without paying taxes. The new king replaced him with a hard-nosed, letter-of-the-law Chief-of-Customs, Charles Paxton. Paxton had no qualms about breaking down doors to get at smuggled goods — and he could not be bribed.

"I am determined to my dying day to oppose with all my power all such instruments of slavery and villany," James Otis Jr. barked at Chief Justice Hutchinson as he sat on the bench in the Town House (Old

State House) not far from George Hewes' cobbler shop. The court-room was packed with spectators, anxious to hear Otis challenge his hated foe the Chief Justice, who was sitting on his first case as judge. Only one shy, *"cupid-like"* young attorney was taking notes. *"Otis is a great whale of a man,"* he wrote, *"with little eyes and a big mouth. . . . He is extremely quick and elastic, his apprehensions as quick as his temper. . . He displayed so comprehensive a knowledge upon the subject, he showed not only the illegality of the Writs, but he laid open the views and designs of Great Britain in taxing us; of destroying our Charters and assuming the powers of our Government. . ."* Otis continued speaking for four hours, from early afternoon until candles had to be called for to light the room. The short, plump attorney, hardly able to see to take the notes, was John Adams of Braintree. He records that Otis spoke of *"the natural rights of mankind,"* and that *"taxation without representation is tyranny. . . . He performed with such a profusion of learning, such a convincing argument and such a torrent of sublime eloquence, that a great crowd of spectators and auditors went away electrified."* Judge Hutchinson made no decision on the enforcement of the Writs of Assistance that day, but postponed his decision until, he said, *"I can hear from England."* A few months later, word came from England that Otis had lost the court case, but he had never expected to win. Hutchinson, in his Journal, summarized the meaning of it all when he wrote: *"From so small a spark a great fire seems to have been kindled."*

John Adams, who joined the Whig Party against the loyalist Tories, stimulated by Otis' oratory, shortly thereafter described Otis as *"bully-ing, bantering, reproaching, ridiculing,"* with, *"no politeness, no delacacy, no taste and no sense."* He came to these conclusions after listening to Otis' unceasing chatter at the Whig Club meetings, held at the Royal Coffee House in downtown Boston. Adams was a virtuous young man who seemed to find fault with everyone and everything. *"Young gentlemen take every evening in this Town; playing cards, drinking punch and wine, smoking tobacco, and swearing."* In the taverns, where most political meetings were held, he concluded, *"dis-eases, vicious habits, bastards and legislators are frequently begotten."*

One disease, supposedly begotten in the taverns of Boston, was smallpox, which raged as an epidemic in 1763. A 22 year old chunky but handsome doctor, Joseph Warren, a member of the Whig Party, was one of the few people John Adams seemed to admire. He first met with the doctor when he went to see him at his house near Faneuil Hall to be inoculated against smallpox. It was the witty and persuasive doctor who also convinced Adams that the real disease in Boston was British tyranny. Among Doctor Warren's other patients were George Hewes, Paul Revere, John Hancock and Chief Justice Hutchinson. It was Warren who started the Liberty Party, which Adams, Revere, Hancock and Hewes joined, it being even more liberal and radical than the Whigs in opposing British taxes, restrictions and laws. Warren, however, first became famous in Boston by insisting that people should be inoculated to avoid being stricken by the deadly smallpox. When George Hewes was inoculated he refused to obey the doctor who insisted he diet on water to avoid a reaction and possible death from the inoculation. He was not to eat or drink anything for 24 hours. *"I stole a roast veal from the larder of the house where I lodged,"* he later admitted, *"and dipped it in a pot of melted butter."* His friend and fellow lodger Ben Ross, who was also inoculated, was starving too and wanted a piece of the meat George had stolen. *"I refused,"* said George, *"suicide is enough for me, but not murder."* Pain gripped George's stomach almost immediately after eating the meat and Ben Ross ran for the nearest doctor. George was sick for days but he didn't get the pox.

That same year Bostonians voted in James Otis Jr. as a representative to the Massachusetts General Court, and British Parliament passed a new tax law on the importation of sugar to the colonies, *"to defray necessary expenses of defending, protecting and securing said colonies."* Otis was outspoken against this new tax. He wrote a booklet *"The Rights of the British Colonies Asserted and Proved,"* again emphasizing that Britain had no right to tax America, and that in the process she was destroying American trade. Parliament passed another devastating tax ten months later called the *"Stamp Act,"* which required Americans to use tax-stamps on pamphlets, newspapers, deeds, licenses and all documents and other legal papers. Some of the stamps were to cost as much as twenty shillings apiece.

At the time, however, George Hewes had other more important things on his mind than taxes. Being a bachelor he needed to hire a washerwoman to do his laundry, and he decided to visit his neighbor Mrs. Sumner who lived by Mill Pond to see if one of her six pretty daughters might be willing to wash his clothes each week. The smallest of the lot, *"sweet Sally,"* obliged him. Week after week for two years, George visited the Sumner home to collect his clean wash and to pay Sally. Mr. Sumner, who was the church sexton and as George relates, *"spoke hard and quick like the tick of a cobbler's hammer,"* was well aware that George wasn't hanging around his house to watch his clothes dry. One evening he approached Mr. Sumner to say, *"I'd like to take your daughter's hand in marriage, if I may have the liberty of the house. "* The old man, as gruff as ever, shouted, *"You've been taking the liberty of the house for two years, and now you come and ask for it? "* — but he finally gave George permission to marry Sally. George's first indication of what Otis was shouting about all this time, was when he was told he would have to pay a hefty tax to England to get the marriage certificate.

The Stamp Act passed into law in Parliament on March 22, 1765 but was not to go into effect in the Colonies until November 1st. The British hoped to receive some 60,000 pounds sterling each year from the Americas through the new tax. In April, John Hancock wrote a letter to a friend in the British Parliament saying that he considered the Stamp Act *"to be very cruel — We were before much burthened, but we shall not much longer be able to support trade, and in the end Great Britain must feel the ill effects of it. . . We are now groaning under the load of debts. "* All of America, but especially New England was in a depression, yet during and right after the French and Indian War, business had been booming. All of the imposed British taxes, most believed, were the cause of the depression, and restrictions on American trade and manufacturing by Britain's Parliament, caused food and clothes prices to go up. Seamen and dock workers, some 12,000, were unemployed — for them and the merchants, the new Stamp Act was the last straw. John Adams wrote in his diary: *"This year brings ruin or salvation to the British Colonies. The eyes of all America are fixed on the British Parliament. . . In short, Britain and America are staring at each other. "* All Americans blamed Parliament and the King's Ministers, but not the King himself. *"The King, it is said is sick, insaine, and could not write his name to sign the Act, "* wrote Adams. *"The people here are restless and group on street corners. . . . and get into fist fights. "* Doctor Warren wrote a letter which was published in the *Boston Gazette* — *"Awake, awake my countrymen, and by a regular and legal opposition, defeat the designs of those who would enslave us and our property. . . . Mortals yet unborn will bless your generous efforts and revere the memory of the saviours of their country. . . I exhort you against promoting by any ways or means whatsoever, the operation of this grevious and burdensome law. "* The popular street ballad of the day, sung in chorus on street corners, taverns and pubs was *"The Tax Song. "*

"They're going to tax the brandy, ale and whiskey, rum and wine,
They'll tax the tea and sugar, the tobacco, snuff and pipes.
They're going to tax the fish that swim and all the birds that fly,
And they're going to tax the women who go drinking on the sly. "

Banks were closing, shops were being boarded up, vessels were rotting at the docks, and the unemployed dockworkers, teamsters and mechanics were restless and angry— Boston was a powderkeg, ready to explode. The Suffolk County Sheriff and the ten constables of Boston were frightened, for they knew they couldn't control the thousands of *"bullyboys"* of Boston, who every year on November 5th, would parade the streets carrying clubs and effigies of the Pope and the Devil — running roughshod over the town. *"Pope's Day,"* also called *"Guy Fawkes Day,"* was when the gang from the North End of Boston would meet the gang from the South End on the Common and at the bridge near Mill Pond, where they would fight to get control of *"a gigantic figure made of wood, paper and straw, representing the Devil, a hideous form with a pitchfork in his hand and covered with tar and feathers."* This annual celebration of marching, singing, and public drinking would inevitably turn nasty when darkness and drunkeness set in. *"Guy Fawkes Day,"* however, was much like Halloween is celebrated today, with children in masks, blackened faces and costumes going door to door carrying jack-o'-lanterns and trick or treating. They recited poems, such as, *"The fifth of November, as you will remember, was gunpowder, treason and plot. I know of no reason why the gunpowder treason should ever be forgot."* Guy Fawkes, a Catholic, had tried to blow up the King, and was caught in the act of stealing the gunpowder. He supposedly confessed that the Pope was behind the plot, but this was only part of the reason for the celebration. During the day of November 5th, a disguised man wearing a mask and heavy jack-boots entered town riding an ass, and would invite children to follow, as fifers and drummers danced around him. He was called *"Joyce Junior"* after a soldier named George Joyce, who had captured the hated King Charles I, and then, wearing a mask, was given the honor of chopping off the king's head — therefore, the wild and boisterous holiday also had an anti-Crown flavor to it. People had been maimed for life and killed during the wild festivities, and in 1765, Guy Fawkes Day was to be celebrated four days after the new Stamp Act was to go into effect. George Hewes, always ready to let off a little steam, was looking forward to it — he always brought along his heel-tapping hammer to the Common when celebrating Guy Fawkes Day.

One Southender who enjoyed helping in the planning and chorus singing of the day was Sam Adams, cousin of John but 13 years his elder. Sam didn't like all the fighting though, and considered it a waste of good energy. He realized that the real enemy wasn't the North Boston folks, but the aristocratic Tories who were pawns of the British government. Sam was mild mannered, fun-loving, and slow moving, but he also was a fierce activist. He was a widower, unemployed, and lived on Prosper Street in the South End near the docks with his two children, a black servant girl, and a big shaggy dog. Like John Hancock, he was a Harvard graduate, but unlike Hancock, he had paid his own way through college by waiting on tables, and was considered by his classmates as *"one of the less well to do boys."* After college, he failed at every job he attempted: counting-house clerk, shop-keeper, salesman, and brewer, but he was a Boston selectman and considered one of Boston's leading politicians. He hated rich aristocrats, especially ones like Tom Hutchinson, who, because of his wealth and family name, had become a powerful politician. *"In every country and government,"* said Sam, *"particular men are too rich. . . . and it is a crime to be rich at the public expense."* Sam had many friends and was liked by everyone, even his critical cousin John, who called him *"my brother,"* and like John, he was a virtuous man, and one of the few pure Puritans left in Boston Town. One of Sam's close friends was a fiery, quick tempered Scot named Andrew Mackintosh, leader of the South End gang of bullyboys. Sam talked to him like a father and begged him to make peace with the Northenders, and together, vent their wrath on the real enemy.

The *Massachusetts Gazette* managed to get a hold of a list of the men who the Crown appointed as Stamp Act officials throughout New England. The list was published on the front page of the newspaper, and the name at the head of the list, Andrew Oliver, spurred Sam Adams into action. Oliver was Lieutenant Governor Tom Hutchinson's brother-in-law. Sam gathered his flock, which included the Mackintosh gang, Revere, Hewes and the other Northenders, lawyers, merchants, and even some liberal ministers, who Governor Bernard called *"the black regiment."* Sam also managed to convince his fellow Boston selectman John Hancock to join the crowd of over 1,000 Bostonians to meet at an elm grove, called Hanover Square (now the corner of Essex and Washington Streets) near the Common. They gathered under the spreading branches of the oldest and biggest elm tree, which was named that day *"The Liberty Tree."*

On the morning of the 14th of August, 1765, two effigies were found hanging from the tree branches. One was a straw-and-paper lifesized likeness of Andrew Oliver, identified by a sign which read: *"The Stamp Officer,"* and the other was a large jack-boot with the Devil's head sticking out of it, an obvious leftover from Guy Fawkes Day. By mid-morning most downtown Boston shops were closed and a restless crowd gathered at the elm grove. At noon there were speeches, planned by the master of agitation, Sam Adams. Hearing of this open-air meeting, Hutchinson sent Sheriff Greenleaf to Hanover Square to cut down the effigies, but when the sheriff saw the large excited crowd, he didn't dare cut them down. Later in the day the Mackintosh gang cut down the effigies and layed them on boards to be carried through the streets in a mock funeral, with hundreds of mourners following. With drums beating, they marched to the Old State House where the Governor and his Council were in session, and tramped through the building, shouting in unison, *"Liberty, property, no stamps."* This so unnerved Governor Bernard that he took a boat to the British fort on Castle Island, fearing that this crowd of dock workers, sailors and mechanics would get nasty once darkness set in. The Governor was right, but with Sam Adams' guidance, the terror and destruction inflicted by the mob that night wasn't as bad as anticipated: A little wooden building under construction as the new Stamp Office was torn apart, and was taken piece by piece to Fort Hill, near Andrew Oliver's mansion, and became part of a large bonfire, as did the effigies. Then, as the *Boston News Letter* reported, *"The populace after this went to work on the barn, fence, garden, and dwelling house of the gentleman, Andrew Oliver."* As the occupants fled, many entered the house and drank some of Oliver's wine, broke a few windows then left. Said one eyewitness, *"they would not have entered his house had it not been for some irritating language from within,"* but all in all, it was a peaceful demonstration for the *"bullyboys."* However, they returned to Oliver's house the following night, built another bonfire, and were intent on further damage to Oliver's property, when word came to them from one of his servants that he was writing to England that very night to resign his position as stamp officer. After a few *"Huzzas"* for Oliver, the crowd dispersed.

Governor Bernard offered 100 pounds sterling as a reward for any information on individuals who caused the disturbance at Oliver's home, but as hard up for cash as Bostonians were, no information or names were given to Bernard. *"The troubles of this country take their rise from and owe their continuance to one man,"* wrote the Governor to England's Earl of Shelbourne, *"and this man is James Otis. He is by nature a passionately violent and desperate man, which qualities sometimes work him up to an absolute frenzy."* To cool this *"frenzy"* and hopefully squelch young Otis' rebellion, he finally gave James Otis Senior a government job. This, to the surprise of Bostonians, turned young Otis around and he announced publicly that *"Parliament has the right to tax, internal and external on lands as well as trade,"* and he told the people to *"treat the new stamp commissioners with respect."* The people replied to his public reversal with a new street-corner jingle:

"Jimmy rallied at upper folks when Jimmy's dad was out. But Jimmy's dad has now a place, so Jimmy's turned about." John Adams was so angry that he wouldn't talk to Otis nor acknowledge his presence when he was in the same room. Cousin Sam, however, spent many hours convincing Otis that not only would the Stamp Act mean ruination to American trade, but would affect lawyers most of all, for all legal papers would require a stamp. He finally convinced Otis that the Stamp Act was bad and the great orator did another turnabout. It is suspected that Sam may have revealed to Otis his and Doc Warren's ultimate plan; the complete separation of America from England. Few, but Adams and Warren, saw or planned beyond the present turmoil created by the Stamp Act, but their mutual goal, taken step by step, was all out revolution, and both Adams and Warren have often been referred to as *"Father of the American Revolution."* As Warren secretly built the foundation and communication network for his *"Liberty Party"* and *"Committees of Safety,"* Sam Adams organized the external forces, with three necessary ingredients — the muscle power from Mackintosh, the money from Hancock, and a needed loud voice. Sam himself was an effective speaker, but his body and voice trembled when he spoke, for he suffered from palsy — there was no one man in the colonies, so eloquent, loud, and effective on his feet than Jimmy Otis. Adams needed him.

It is interesting that, as frightened as Governor Bernard was of the mobs and the growing anarchy, he realized there was an organization behind it all, and that the aim was the overthrow of the British government, but he thought that Otis was the leader, not Sam Adams and Joe Warren. *"The Stamp Act let loose all the ill humor of the common people,"* he wrote to London in 1765, *"and put them into the hands of designing men... The opposing of the Stamp Act had been made a mask for a battery, a stalking horse to take a better aim at the royalty of the government... It was the general opinion that Otis himself wished that the Act might not be repealed as that would answer his inflammatory purposes better."*

On August 26, twelve days after Oliver's estate was visited by the mob, a small bonfire was started at twilight on King Street (now State Street) in front of the Old State House. *"It was so hot out you couldn't breathe,"* said one bystander, so the fire attracted many who couldn't understand having a bonfire on such a hot night. One of the Boston constables came to investigate, but he was stoned by some angry men who had gathered there and he retreated. Someone in the group suggested they go to Mr. Paxton's house, and once there, the hated chief customs officer was wise enough to have a friend invite all the men to a nearby tavern, shouting *"drinks on me,"* and they all followed. Judge William Story, Registrar of the Admiralty lived close by, and after a few mugs of rum, the ever increasing mob moved on to Story's house. He wasn't at home so they broke some windows, then broke down the front door and invaded his wine cellar. Hooting and hollering, the mob, now led by Mackintosh, went to another customs official's house, which they invaded and robbed. Then they headed for Tom Hutchinson's mansion. Hearing the mob approach, Hutchinson and his two sons barricaded windows and doors, and sent his daughters and their servant quickly off to a neighbor's house. When the mob broke in the front door, Hutchinson and his sons also ran to the neighbor's house. Some of the mob chased the lieutenant governor, threatening to kill him, but he managed to escape. His home, however, was devastated. As the *News Letter* reported next day, *"the mob destroyed, carried away, or cast into the street, everything that was in the house and demolished every part of it, except the walls."* Hutchinson appeared at Court the following morning wearing a torn shirt. *"Excuse my appearance,"* he apologized to his fellow judges, *"I have no other garment,"* and he broke down and cried. Mackintosh and eight other North and Southend leaders were arrested and thrown in jail, but Sam Adams warned the authorities that if they weren't released, worse havoc might result — Mackintosh and the others were freed.

The *Massachusetts Gazette* called the destruction of Hutchinson's house *"the lawless ravages of some foreign villains, who took advantage of the over-heated temper of a few people of this place,"* and a few weeks later rallied the forces once more by headlining; *"Shall we not all, as one man, unite in opposing the Act and spill the last drop of our blood if necessity should require, rather than live to see it take place in America?"* Sam Adams wrote many stirring articles for the *Gazette* under the pseudonyms *"Sincerus, Populas,"* and *"A. Puritan."* In one, he warns the public, *"November is very nigh. Let not your courage cool, nor your resentment fail. Love your liberty, and fight for it, like men who know the value of it.... Any merchant clearing out his vessel upon Stamp papers shall meet with our highest displeasure.... I do say, I won't buy one shilling worth of anything that comes from Old England till the Stamp Act is appealed."* This suggestion to boycott all English goods spread throughout New England like wild-fire, and the people, all but the Tories, decided to eat no lamb for a year, which would increase local wool production so New Englanders wouldn't be forced to buy woolen clothes manufactured in England. The Adams cousins, John Hancock, and James Otis were elected to the Massachusetts House of Representatives that year, and they called for a Stamp Act

Congress of all Thirteen Colonies. They met from October 7 through 25 at New York, and all agreed not to import British goods, nor pay taxes imposed by the British government. They also drafted a letter to the King asserting their loyalty and their respect for Parliament, but demanding trials by jury, freedom of taxes imposed by England, and *"relief from the present Stamp Act burden."* Ironically, the Stamp Act brought the Thirteen Colonies together, for prior to this meeting, they always competed, and colonial leaders were jealous and distrustful of each other. The Stamp Act and Sam Adams united them.

Following Boston's example, almost every village and town in New England had a Liberty Tree, and if there was not an appropriate large tree near the center of town, the people erected Liberty Poles. When November 1st rolled around, dock workers refused to load or unload cargoes, shops were closed, church bells rang, and every flag and ship ensign was flown at half mast. At Boston the blood-red stamps were delivered from Halifax and deposited at Castle Island, but Governor Bernard didn't dare have his customs men bring them into port. In other towns, if the stamps could be confiscated by the Liberty Boys, they were, and then they were burned in great bonfires. In retaliation, government officials closed all the courts, for the law was that no legal business could be transacted without the stamps. Governor Bernard wrote to his friends in British Parliament: *"I am at the mercy of the mob. The power and authority of the government is really at an end."*

On November 5th, Guy Fawkes Day, the people of Boston feared the worst. Shops and homes were shut up and barricaded for protection against the North and Southend bully boys, but the suspected riot did not transpire, thanks to Sam Adams. He convinced both groups to meet in peace at a great feast on Boston Common. Mackintosh, who many Bostonians considered *"a cruel mobster,"* pranced about singing and drinking, wearing a red and blue uniform and a gold tri-cornered hat, presented to him by Sam Adams, paid for by John Hancock. The traditional effigies, and a few stamps that someone managed to get their hands on, were added to a bonfire, and everything was peaceful and jovial — all the free food and liquid refreshment was paid for by Hancock. This was to be their *"fun day"* Adams explained to the 2,000 or more celebrants, but they were to meet again at the Liberty Tree in eleven days to transact some business.

On the 16th of November, the 2,000 gathered again under the spreading branches of the tree. Adams and Hancock, one dressed in a shabby brown suit and the other in a gold laced waist coat with ruffles, had persuaded Justice Dana to be with them. The judge was there to administer an oath to Andrew Oliver, who, Adams discovered, had changed his mind again and had told the Governor that he would be the stamp officer. Trembling, Oliver was brought before the people and made to raise his right hand. *"I have never taken any measures to act in the office of stamp-master, and I will never do so directly or indirectly,"* he swore. To seal the oath, Hancock allowed Oliver a pinch of snuff from the gold box he had gotten from King George. Adams then reminded the people not to buy any food or other goods made in England. The people cheered, and then, as John Adams relates, *"on the signal of a whistle, the crowd quickly disappeared into the back streets."* A few days later, a committee comprising of John Adams, James Otis and Jerry Gridley, was sent to Governor Bernard to convince him to allow business transactions without using the stamps. *"If you do not comply,"* said Adams, *"some two-hundred and fifty thousand people of this Province will be on you."* Otis was drunk, and weeping he shouted, *"When the King closes the courts, he unkings himself. Nothing warrants it but war, invasion, rebellion and insurrection...."* and he slurred on for fifteen minutes, but Bernard was an immovable force. *"Tell it to the Judges,"* was his reply. There were no business transactions and little activity during that terribly cold winter and early spring of 1765-66. Paul Revere, for one, was so deep in debt that he almost had to spend the winter in jail.

It was one of John Hancock's smuggling sea captains, Shub Coffin in the brig **HARRISON** that brought in the most unbelievable news from England on Friday, May 16th — Parliament had repealed the Stamp Act. Cannons roared at Castle Island as dock workers spread the news through town, church bells peeled, and people ran into the streets, shouting and dancing. Hancock, Warren, Otis and the Adams cousins couldn't believe their ears. Captain Coffin explained to Hancock that the boycott of English goods had forced the Crown to drop all stamp taxes. British merchants had suffered such losses that they petitioned Parliament *"to secure us from impending ruin, or a multitude of English manufacturers will become a burden on the community, or seek their bread in other countries, to the irretrievable loss of this kingdom"* — British Parliament had no option but to repeal the Act. Monday, March 19th was decided on as the day of celebration, yet many Tories and government officials still feared retaliation from the bullyboys, and although a couple of effigies of customs officials were hung on the Liberty Tree, and a few house windows were broken, it was a day and night of all out gaiety. *"I had not seen anything like it before,"* said George Hewes. As early as one am. Monday morning, church bells started ringing, drummers and fluters marched through the town, wine flowed like water, houses were lit up with candles, and people danced in the streets. The Liberty Tree was decorated with lanterns, *"til its boughs could hold no more,"* and the Liberty Boys sponsored a fireworks display on the Common. *"Rockets, beehives, and serpents played in every quarter,"* said Hewes, *"and to crown all, a magnificent illuminated paper pyramid was erected on the Common, then moved to the Liberty Tree, but the pyramid caught fire from the fireworks and burned."* Paul Revere tacked a copper plaque he made to the trunk of the Liberty Tree, it read *"To Every Lover Of Liberty — August 14, 1765,"* commemorating the day Oliver's house was ransacked. That night, Otis had an open house at his home, Warren sponsored a banquet at the Royal Coffee House, and Hancock had a Madeira wine party for everyone in front of his house. Hewes decided to go to Hancock's party *"where barrels were rolled onto the Common for all to partake."* It was a great evening of *"festivals and demonstrations, even the country people were in town,"* and at one point, *"subscriptions were raised to release those who were in jail for debt,"* John Hancock being the largest contributor. Hewes stumbled home to his in-laws' house in the wee hours of Tuesday morning. He was tipsy and happy — but the party was over. In the Dawn of a new day, the Liberty Party leaders realized that Parliament hadn't repealed what they called, *"The Declaratory Act,"* which allowed England to continue making restrictive laws and taxes on the rebellious Americans.

George Hewes   *Paul Revere*

Sam Adams

John Adams

Joe Warren

Jim Otis

John Hancock

Tom Hutchinson

Photos of portraits, courtesy of the John Hancock Mutual Life Insurance Company, Boston, and the Essex Institute, Salem, MA.

II
THE PARTY'S OVER

"Every man in England seems to consider himself as a piece of a sovereign over America; seems to jostle himself into the throne with the King, and talks of Our Subjects in the Colonies," wrote Ben Franklin from England in 1767. One of Ben's English colleagues who considered himself Lord and Master over the Americans was Charles Townshend, better known as *"Champagne Charlie."* Due to the death of the King's Chancellor of the Exchequer in 1767, Townshend was appointed to that illustrious position. *"The Colonists are doing nothing to help the Empire,"* he told the King and Parliament, *"and I know a mode of revenue that may be drawn from them without offense."* The Townshend Acts, that went into effect in November of that year, were new taxes on glass, paint, lead, paper and tea, which proved to be very offensive to the Americans. Tacked onto the Acts by Parliament was the establishment of a new Board of five Customs Commissioners, to be stationed in Boston to collect import duties on these items. When they arrived in Boston, they were so mistreated by the Liberty Boys that they and their families had to move to Castle Island. In an attempt to stop the rampant smuggling, the customs officers seized one of John Hancock's cargo vessels moored at his wharf, but not in time to confiscate the cargo of Madeira wine that John had snuck into the port without paying taxes to the Crown. Hancock's **LIBERTY** was towed to the 50-gun British warship **ROMNEY** that was anchored off shore, and John Hancock was arrested. When the customs men returned to Hancock Wharf after turning the **LIBERTY** over to the commander of the **ROMNEY**, they were attacked and beaten up by a mob of dock workers, and were forced to retreat to Castle Island to lick their wounds. The boat of one of the customs officials was carried through the streets to Boston Common and, outside Hancock's house, was ripped apart and torched. Hancock was bailed out of jail by John Adams, but was given a heavy fine and the British Navy kept his sloop.

Sam Adams activated his bullyboys again, North and South united, as the *"Sons of Liberty."* They paraded up and down in front of Governor Bernard's house, shouting, whistling and drumming, *"making great noise and hallooing,"* wrote Bernard. He complained to the King, demanding troops *"to control the mobs that rule this Towne."* The Governor now realized who the ringleader was and he publicly called Sam Adams, *"Chief of this tribe of Mohawks."* Sam took the intended slur with a chuckle, and later would spoof the Governor's comment by having his men disguise themselves as Mohawk Indians.

"He is a grand incendiary, " cried Lieutenant Governor Hutchinson, *"the master of puppets. "* To further resist the Townshend Acts, Sam and Joe Warren asked all New Englanders to refuse the importation and consumption of any goods from England that were taxed, and encouraged the manufacture of such items here in America. The merchant mariners were asked to acquire needed and desired items from other foreign nations. Most of them signed a *"non-importation agreement, "* refusing to bring English goods into American ports. *"Those who do not agree, "* Sam warned, *"will be dealt with accordingly. "*

One Boston sea merchant and shop owner, Theophilus Lilly, refused to follow the dictates of his fellow merchants, not only shipping in taxable items from England, but selling them in his downtown shop. Coming to work one morning, Lilly discovered a large canvas head stuffed with straw, sitting on a pole in front of his shop, and the face painted on it was a likeness of himself. There was a large finger and a cartoon of a man's rear-end painted on his front door, and a group of boys — *"wharf-rats, "* gathered outside his shop to taunt him. A neighbor of Lilly's, Ebenezer Richardson, who worked in the Customs House and was known for his Tory tendencies, attempted to chase the boys away from Lilly's shop. The gathering crowd turned on him, calling him *"a British informer, "* and *"Lilly-livered, "* thus coining a new phrase for the word *"coward. "* Richardson was so mad that he tried to make a teamster run the boys over with his horse and cart. The boys started throwing *"filth and stones"* at him until he retreated into his house, and then they bombarded his house with similar ammunition. Richardson grabbed his musket and fired out a second story window, wounding a teenager named Christopher Gore, and killing a twelve year old German boy named Chris Snider. Adults soon arrived with cutlasses and muskets, bent on hanging Richardson, but he was saved from execution by four constables who dragged him off to jail. The wounded boy was rushed to Doc Warren's home, where a musket-ball was removed from his leg. Christopher Gore, later became Governor of Massachusetts.

Young Chris Snider was set in a coffin under the Liberty Tree — carved into the coffin were the words *"Innocence Itself Not Safe. "* A funeral procession led by the boy's family and Joseph Warren was followed by 34 carts, chariots, and coaches and 1,500 marchers, including some 500 schoolboys. On the day of the funeral, the *Massachusetts Gazette* headlined: *"This innocent lad was the first whose life has been a victim to the cruelty and rage of oppressors, for, young as he was, he died in his country's cause. . ."* — It seems that Adams and Warren were recruiting boys as well as men to their cause of Liberty. Lt. Govvernor Hutchinson called the boy's death *"justifiable manslaughter,"* and Richardson received only two years in jail.

Governor Bernard's wish came true. In response to his request for troops, eight British warships and seven troop-ships entered Boston Harbor, to a reception of fireworks provided by the customs officials and their families at Castle Island. *"They came up the harbour and anchored round the Towne as for a regular seige. . . ."* wrote Paul Revere on September 30th, 1768. *"At noon next day, the 14th and 29th regiments and a detachment from the 59th regiment, and a train of artillary landed on Long Wharf; there formed and marched with insolent parade, drums beating, fifes playing, up King Street. . ."* George Hewes, hammer in hand, rushed from his shop to watch them too. The crowd of Bostonians that gathered was silent, but for a few rude remarks. Little boys danced in and out of the ranks shouting, *"Lobster-backs,"* and *"Lobsters for sale."* George saw the smiles on a few Tory faces, but otherwise there were no incidents nor challenges by the Liberty Boys in the crowd. George and Paul Revere both noticed that the Brown Bess muskets that the Redcoats carried were loaded and ready to fire, *"and each had 16 extra rounds of ammunition ready."* The soldiers didn't have any trouble from the Liberty Boys that day, but they did have trouble finding places to sleep that night. The British officers went to John Hancock, among others, in hopes he would provide warehouses to quarter the soldiers, but John and the others who owned warehouses refused. For the next few nights, the Redcoats slept in the Old State House, Faneuil Hall, and in tents on Boston Common. When British General Thomas Gage, Commander-in-Chief of the Army, arrived a few days later, he forced the residents of Boston to take soldiers into their homes until barracks could be built. The General himself stayed with the Shaw family, neighbors of Paul Revere, who were fiercely anti-British. James Otis commented that he was glad to see the Redcoats out of the Old State House where the General Court sat, *"for the soldiers smell."* The ill-fed, poorly paid soldiers were mostly recruits from the slums of England, Ireland and Wales, *"a surley lot,"* said Otis, who realized right from the start that they were not welcome in Boston Towne.

On the night of their arrival the Sons of Liberty met at Bill Molineaux's hardware store to decide whether or not they should arm themselves — and begin the war right then and there — or just harrass the troops until the colonies could build up a bigger and better supply of arms and ammunition. Molineaux, a hot-tempered Irishman, wanted *"war now."* Adams and Warren, however, prevailed on the group to agree on *"non-cooperation with the British Army,"* for the time being.

"The mobs have been put in their place by the gallant British soldiers," wrote one Tory, but night after night during the following year there were brawls between Liberty Boys and soldiers on the streets and in the taverns. A few Redcoats had been thrown off wharfs and two were drowned in Mill Pond. Sam Adams fed the flames of hatred toward the occupying British military by occasionally writing articles for the *Massachusetts Gazette* under one of his many aliases: *"Redcoats are beating up small boys and forcing our local girls to bed with them,"* he said in one article, *"a poor old man went insane when he discovered his innocent grand-daughter in bed with a British soldier,"* he wrote in another. The soldiers, having much spare time on their hands sometimes wrote articles in response to Sam's propaganda, which often helped fan the flames for Sam. In one retort, soldiers of the 29th regiment, mostly Dublin boys, wrote *"The Puritan girls of Boston aren't that pure."* which enraged the populace. Even Lt. Governor Hutchinson said that the 29th were *"bad fellows, and it seems impossible to restrain them."* One of their officers, Major John Pitcairn, wrote to the Earl of Sandwich that *"I have lived almost every day and night amongst the men for these five or six weeks past, on purpose to keep them from the pernicious rum. The rum is so cheap here that it debauches both navy and army, and kills many of them. Depend on it, my Lord, and it will destroy more of us than the Yankees will."* General Gage attempted to stop the fights, drunkeness and womanizing of his men by calling for an 8 p.m. curfew for soldiers and civilians. This seemed to work temporarily but Adams was always looking for new angles. Strangely enough, the people of Boston liked General Gage, and many commented how much he looked like Sam Adams — *"enough to be his twin,"* some said. Sam couldn't see any resemblance.

As darkness set in around Boston, British soldiers on guard duty often challenged civilians to stop and be recognized, and then questioned them as to why they were out at night. One British soldier ordered Doc Warren to stop as he hurriedly walked the streets to see an ailing patient. Warren didn't stop or answer the soldier's question of, *"Who goes there?"* He grabbed Warren by the collar, but the Doctor knocked him down and quickly walked on. George Hewes was also caught out in the streets after the curfew one night. Two Redcoat sentries caught him sneaking down a back alley towards home. *"Who goes there?"* shouted one. *"What's the countersign?"* roared the other. George didn't reply, but reached into his coat and took out a bottle of rum. *"This is my counter sign,"* he said, handing the bottle to the Redcoats, *"and I'm going nowhere."* As Hewes relates, *"the vigilant Dublin Dogberrys both got drunk, and when they were discovered by their superior officer, both got 300 lashes of the whip apiece."* Many British soldiers came to Hewes to have him make them shoes, and one whom he befriended, Private Burke, got the shoes but didn't pay for them. George went to see his superior officer, Captain Preston, after waiting three months for his payment. Preston assured Hewes that he would take care of it. The next thing George knew, Burke sent him a note inviting him to his punishment of *"300 lashes of the whip."* Hewes didn't go to Burke's whipping, but said, *"If I knew he would be punished so severely, I would have been quiet about the shoes."* Another British soldier caught stealing from a local shop was given a punishment of 1,000 lashes, but he didn't live through it. Two others were caught breaking into a shop in the night time— they were hanged on Boston Common. It's no wonder there were so many desertions from the Army once the troops landed in Boston. Over 50 of them had disappeared into the countryside before they were here two weeks. Always on the lookout for recruits, Adams and Warren set up a *"safe-house"* for British Army deserters in the Black Horse Tavern on Salem Street, where they were not only given refuge but also converted to the cause of Liberty.

Because British officers and their Boston Tory friends began frequenting the Royal Coffee House, the Whigs moved to Salutation Tavern on North Street, an old hangout for Boston mechanics. It was here that Warren organized the mechanics into his *"Committee of Safety,"* with Paul Revere as their leader. They were not only to be messengers, delivering news and instructions to Liberty Boys in other towns and villages, but they were trained as spies, constantly gathering information on British supplies, weapons and troop movements. The one problem with this first American spy-ring was that one of its own members was spying on them and delivering information on their activities to Hutchinson and to General Gage. *"We were so careful that our meetings be kept secret,"* said Revere, *"that everytime we met, every person swore upon the Bible that they would not discover any of our transactions."* Paul Revere and Joe Warren realized there was a turncoat informer in their midst, but they didn't know who he was — George Washington accidentally discovered him, months after the Battle of Bunker Hill, when the American Army was camped at Cambridge. Revere finally decided that their secret meetings at Salutation Tavern were vulnerable to detection from outsiders, so he moved the meetings to the Green Dragon Tavern on Union Street, with a slinky copper dragon sign over the door. Important Liberty Party meetings were also held there and on King Street, at The Bunch Of Grapes Tavern, where patriotism and punch went hand in hand.

There were about two hundred pubs and taverns in Boston at the time, one for every 200 of the 20,000 men, women and children who lived in Boston. Sam Adams enjoyed telling the story of The King's Arms Tavern and The King's Head Tavern, which were located on opposite street corners in downtown Boston. *"A British officer asked me the other day, where he might drink, sup, and sleep for the night,"* said Sam to his colleges, *"so I told him, 'Sir, the King's Arms is full, so I suggest you go to the King's Head, for the King's Head is empty'. "*

The ever changeable, moody and nervous Jimmy Otis enjoyed eating and drinking everywhere. Even though the British had taken over the Royal Coffee House, he still enjoyed their special sour-beer and rum drink mix called a *"Whistle Belly Vengeance, "* so he continued to frequent the place. As John Adams reveals in his diary, *"Otis would tell offcolor jokes about Old Horn, a horny old lawyer, "* and many proper Bostonians at the Royal Coffee House considered his stories disgusting. *"Old Horn overtook a pretty young maiden riding a bony mare to market out by the neck,"* Otis boomed as he swilled his rum drinks. *"Old Horn asked to let him Jigg her. 'What's Jigging?' she asked, 'What good will it do?' Old Horn replied, 'It will make you fat' 'Pray be so good then' says the maiden 'to Jigg my horse, for she is miserably lean.'"* Otis would laugh the loudest at his own jokes, and tankards would be lifted to toast Old Horn. On one cool September evening in 1769, at the Royal Coffee House, as Otis, *"in his cups, "* spewed forth one joke after another about Old Horn to the entertainment of British officers and Tories, John Robinson, one of the new Customs Commissioners, questioned Jimmy's loyalty to the King. Otis demanded an apology from him. He loved the King, but to him, *"the King's men are thieves and villains. "* Some of the British officers sitting with Robinson, jumped up, knocking over their table, drawing their swords and cutlasses. Robinson and Otis went for each others throats, tipping over more tables and flicking out all the candles in the room. In the darkness, men groped for each other — it was a blind free-for-all with fists, swords, canes and cutlasses swinging. Otis got the worst of it, and when the candles were relit, he was found moaning on the floor of the Coffee House, bleeding profusely from *"a great crack in his skull"* — he had been hacked by a cutlass. He was rushed to Joe Warren's house, but the wound was so deep that *"it penetrated his skull"* said Warren. Warren bandaged him up, but Otis was never right in the head again. Warren went to the Coffee House and demanded a fight with Robinson, but Robinson swore it wasn't he who struck Otis with the cutlass, and he refused to fight Warren. When Jimmy's wound healed but he didn't, John Rowe, a local merchant, who had also fought with a British officer at the Royal Coffee House, wrote in his diary that, *"Otis got into a mad freak tonight and broke a great many windows in the State House.* " A few days later, Rowe reveals, *"Otis behaved very madly, firing guns out of his windows, and he raved against his wife.* " Jimmy's wife Ruth was an avid Tory, a beautiful and wealthy woman, but as John Adams hints in his diary, *"she wasn't fond of her husband's speeches.* " Realizing that her husband was not to recover his sanity, she had friends tie him up after one of his wild rages, and she carted him off to the village of Andover. There, he spent some ten years *"becoming very plump"* and occasionally writing anti-British articles for the newspapers, which he signed *"Mister Oates.* " Sitting out on his front porch in Andover one day in 1780, he was struck by a bolt of lightning and killed. He never did see the victorious end to the seemingly impossible struggle that he had started.

Another key figure in the struggle, who left the scene about the same time Otis was carted out of Boston, was Governor Sir Francis Bernard. He had done everything in his power to control the mobs of Boston and to stem the tide of liberty. He had called in the army, refused to allow the lower House of Representatives, led by Hancock and Adams, to meet, and came close to having Otis, Hancock and Adams *"captured and shipped off to England to hang at Tyburn for treason,"* as many Boston Tories had suggested. The Earl of Sandwich suggested that the Governor be given a baronetcy and recalled to England. The Earl thought that Hutchinson and General Gage would provide tougher resistance to these *"most treacherous, infamous, and worthless race of men on earth,"* than Bernard did. *"The Americans are fanatics,"* wrote the Earl, *"who bluster and swell when danger is at a distance, but when it comes near, will like all other mobs, throw down their arms and run away.* " When Governor Bernard received word that he was to return to England, he was in such a rush to get out of Boston that he departed on the next available vessel, leaving behind all his belongings and his family. At Harvard College, students ruined a fine portrait of the Governor that hung in the college meeting hall, by cutting out a heartshaped piece of the canvas below his smiling face. With Bernard gone, Hutchinson was once again Governor, and he began filling more governmental positions with members of his family. His two sons were made agents of the British East India Company, collecting taxes in America on the importation of tea. Hutchinson's brother-in-law Andrew Oliver, the reluctant stamp tax officer, became Lieutenant Governor.

It was a bright but chilly moonlit night as George Hewes left the Bunch Of Grapes Tavern to hurry home before the curfew. Passing the Old State House, he noticed a young woman turning into Prison Lane. She didn't look like one of the many prostitutes that frequented the area now that neighboring warehouses had been converted into barracks for the British soldiers. Hewes saw that a rough looking British soldier followed her into the dark lane, so George quietly walked up the lane behind them, fearing the soldier was up to no good. George then saw the soldier hit the girl a hard blow to the face with his fist and quickly strip her of her *"bonnet, muff and tippet."* George shouted, and the soldier ran off, carrying her clothes with him. George chased him to the barracks, but was stopped by sentries, which allowed the thief to escape. The sentries did reveal to George that the soldier whom he was chasing was Private Mathew Kilroy of the 29th regiment. Next morning George returned to the barracks and was allowed to confront Kilroy face to face. Kilroy, in his Dublin brogue, denied beating up and robbing the girl. Hewes told him that if he didn't confess and give up the articles of clothing he had stolen, he would go to General Gage and tell him what he saw. Fearing a whipping or worse, Kilroy gave up the items of clothes to Hewes. After Private Burke's heavy punishment for not paying for his shoes, George decided not to report Kilroy to his superior officer. Hewes found the girl and returned the clothes to her, but he was angry at himself for being the good Samaritan, for the girl didn't even thank him.

A few days later, Private Mathew Kilroy was in trouble again. He went to Gray's Ropewalk near the docks looking for part time work, which General Gage had allowed his soldiers to do, for their sixpence a day hardly kept them in spending money. Sam Gray, no relation to the owner but a worker at the ropewalk, told Kilroy he could *"clean out the shit-house."* In response to the comment, Kilroy slugged Gray. Gray and some of the other workers pounced on Kilroy and beat him up. He went back to the barracks and returned to the ropewalk later that day with eleven other soldiers. A donnybrook broke out, but the rope-walkers got the best of the fight and the soldiers retreated. The Redcoats of the 29th regiment then pledged revenge. Sam Adams and Joe Warren heard that they planned to beat up any civilians they found wandering the streets of Boston that following Monday night. A meeting of the Liberty Boys was held and preparations were made to meet that threat.

George Hewes was wandering the streets from tavern to tavern that night. It was cold, with a glaze of ice and snow on the cobblestones and roofs. At about 7 p.m.. he saw a group of fishermen and dockworkers gathered outside Faneuil Hall near Dock Square. A tall man wearing a white powdered wig and red jacket was talking to them, and seemed to be giving them some sort of a pep-talk. George thought it might be the hot-tempered Bill Molineaux disguised as a judge, or as Joyce Junior, who usually didn't appear in public until November 5th — this was only

March 5th. George was too far away to hear what he was saying, but when the strange speaker left, the 60 or more who had gathered, started cheering and yelling. Some of them, George noticed, carried white sticks, which identified them as Liberty Boys. As they marched up the street towards him, church bells started ringing, which usually meant a fire somewhere in town. People started coming out of their houses carrying buckets of water, but there was no redness in the sky, nor was there a smell of smoke. The only fire, George was quick to realize, was in the eyes of the men marching up Dock Square towards King Street. George joined them, for he could tell that, fire or not, there would be a hot time in old Boston Town this night — it was a party George didn't want to miss.

Two young wigmakers, whom George knew, came running down from King Street to meet the crowd. Breathlessly, one said that they had passed a sentry near the Old State House, *"and we remarked about his long hair, so he took a swipe at us with his rifle."* The crowd growled and hurried up the hill toward the State House, the wigmakers following. As they entered King Street, a 13 year old boy stumbled towards them crying. He was Piemont the barber's apprentice. He blubbered to the crowd that the British sentry in his box outside the Custom House had *"cuffed me on the head with the butt of his musket, and I thought I was killed."* As some stopped to inspect the bump on the boy's head, the others moved on past the State House to the tiny sentry box nearby, located outside the Custom House. Private Hugh Montgomery stood in the box, stomping his feet and blowing on his hands to fight the coldness in them, but he grabbed his musket and held it at the ready when he saw the angry mob approach. Leading the mob was a husky mulatto, half black, half Indian, named Crispus Attucks. He carried a club in his hand and waved it in Montgomery's face. *"If you molest me, I will fire,"* Montgomery shouted at Attucks, aiming his musket at him. People in the crowd started shouting profanities at the sentry, and a few threw snowballs at him, which he ducked by retreating into his narrow box. The crowd now had increased in size, the ones in back pushing the ones in front closer to Montgomery. *"Call out the guard,"* he shouted with a shrill voice, over and over again, still aiming his musket at those who hemmed him in. Hewes, being so short, had squeezed through the crowd to the front, so he could see what was going on. He could see that Montgomery was trembling, possibly in a combination of cold, fear, and anger. *"I'll blow your bloody brains out,"* he screamed at Attucks, who was taunting him with his club. *"You do, and you'll swing for it,"* shouted the fat local bookseller Henry Knox, who later became a General in Washington's Army. There was cursing and shouting from the rear of the crowd, and Hewes felt a rifle-butt on his shoulder, shoving him into his neighbor Nat Fosdick. *"Out of the way!"* someone shouted from behind him. *"I move for no man,"* George shouted back, and saw, to his amazement, Private Mathew Kilroy, bullying his way through the crowd with six armed Redcoats following, and Captain Thomas Preston running behind them. As they broke through the crowd, Private Montgomery, for an instant, took his eyes off Attucks. The big mulatto dropped his club and grabbed the sentry's musket. Montgomery wrestled it back and quickly lined up with his fellow Redcoats, their muskets, fixed with bayonets, aimed at the crowd. Snowballs packed with ice, stones and oyster shells started flying through the air and landing on the scarlet coats and pointed hats, one knocking the hat off Captain Preston's head. Preston ordered the Bostonians to move back, but they moved forward. Standing with Hewes and being pushed towards the bayonets by the shouting mob behind them, were Nat Fosdick, Black Peg the local whore, merchant sailor Jim Caldwell, and ropemaker Sam Gray, whom Kilroy had battled with three nights before.

There was no order given, *"just a flash of powder"* from Kilroy's musket, said George, and Sam Gray fell backwards, dead. Then the other Redcoats began firing, point blank into the crowd. Montgomery shot Crispus Attucks in the chest. There were screams and shouts of *"bloody murder,"* as most of the crowd dispersed and fled down adjoining streets and dark alleys. Irishman Patrick Carr was shot in the stomach, and teenager Sam Maverick, another of George's neighbors, had a musketball rip right through him. Jim Caldwell turned and started to run but bumped into George, knocking him over, and then he fell on top of George. *"Get up Jim, get up,"* shouted George in near-panic, struggling to push the sailor off of him. Then George realized that the wetness he felt on his hands wasn't from the snowy street, but was the sticky blood of death — Jim Caldwell had two musket-ball holes in his back. George sat on the wet cobblestones with Caldwell's head cradled in his lap. He saw the Redcoats reload and fire another volley at the fleeing crowd. Then he watched as Private Kilroy stepped forward and thrust his bayonet into the limp body of Samuel Gray.

III
ON THE WARPATH

Five civilians were killed and five wounded by the Redcoats at the Boston Massacre. *"Samuel Gray, in a most peaceable manner, "* said eyewitness Ed Langford, *"without a weapon, not even a snowball, was killed immediately by Private Kilroy's gunfire, and Gray dropped at my left foot."* Richard Palmer, another member of the March 5th mob, said that *"Private Montgomery, after firing his gun at Attucks and killing him, tried to bayonet me."* A few minutes after the Massacre, as more British soldiers swarmed into the streets from the nearby barracks, Nat Appleton who lived in the neighborhood, said that *"Twelve soldiers with bayonets attacked me on the steps of my house, but I managed to get inside and bolt the door."* His teenaged son John testified that he and his nine year old brother, *"while on King Street later that evening, we were attacked by twenty soldiers with knives. One shouted, 'We will kill you all,' and he hit me with a sheathed cutlass."* George Hewes, with the help of Nat Fosdick, had carried Seaman Jim Caldwell's body to the Boston Gaol, and there George informed Caldwell's friend and captain Mat Morton what had happened. *"Morton went mad with rage, "* said George, *"and he left the Gaol shouting that he was going to 'kill a regular before the night was over'."* Peace was restored that evening when Governor Hutchinson, hearing the ruckus and gun shots from his home, arrived on the scene and from the balcony of the State House, begged the angry mob and British soldiers to return to their homes and barracks. He then had Captain Preston and his squad of *"eight killers"* arrested and put in jail.

Next morning, the Boston Town Fathers, led by Sam Adams, insisted that the Governor convince Colonel Dalyrymple to move the British troops out of Boston. Reluctantly, Hutchinson had the Colonel send most of his men to Castle Island. Hutchinson also agreed to a civilian trial with a jury for Preston and his men, but no lawyers in New England could be found to defend them — all feared reprisals from the Sons of Liberty. James Forester, a friend of Captain Preston's, went to Josiah Quincy, a 26 year old cock-eyed attorney from Braintree, and pleaded with him to defend the British Captain and his men. Quincy, who suffered from a tubercular cough, agreed, but only if Forester could persuade John Adams to be the spokesman attorney for the British. Forester, known to his friends as the *"Irish Infant,"* was crying when he approached John Adams to have him defend Captain Preston. John, now married with two children, realized his Liberty Party friends and other Bostonians would criticize him for coming to the aid of the

Massacre Redcoats, but he agreed to join Quincy in defending them in court. Ironically, the attorneys representing the citizens and the Commonwealth were Josiah's brother Samuel Quincy, a Tory, and Robert Treat Paine, a *"bumpy nosed"* Boston lawyer, whom John Adams hated with a passion. As early as February 11, 1759, John had written in his diary, *"Bob Paine and Doctor Wendel took Katy Quincy and Polly Jackson, and led them into a retired room, and there laughed and screamed, and kissed and hussled. They came out glowing like furnaces. . . . Paine thinks himself in high favor with the ladies, but he little thinks how he is blasted sometimes."* The feeling was mutual, for Bob Paine thought John Adams to be *"an imprudent, illbred, conceited fellow."*

John Adams once wrote in his diary, *"How shall I gain a reputation? How shall I spread an opinion of myself as a lawyer of distinguished genius, learning and virtue?"* Defending the Redcoats provided him with his desired fame, but turned most of his friends against him. Boys followed him down the street *"jeering and calling me foul names,"* and at night, they'd throw rocks at his house. *"I am afraid I won't have a friend left,"* he wrote, *"let alone a client. . . I have lost half my business at the bar."* Josiah Quincy received similar treatment. Even his father wrote to him, *"I am under great affliction at hearing the bitterest reproaches uttered against you, for having become an advocate for those criminals. . . . I must own to you, it had filled the bosom of your aged and infirm parent with anxiety and distress."* Josiah replied to his father that, *"these criminals charged with murder, are not yet proved guilty, and therefore, however criminal, are entitled the laws of God and man, to all legal counsel and aid. . . I never harboured the expectation that all men should speak well of me."*

After Adams and Quincy rejected twenty jurors, twelve of them hand-picked by Sam Adams in an attempt to sway the verdict, and two of Hutchinson's judges quit, unable to withstand further harrassment from outspoken Bostonians, Captain Preston's trial was finally slated for early October. The soldiers' trial was set for late November. They were all accused of murder, and all pleaded *"not guilty."* The four judges wore red robes and curly white wigs, signifying a murder trial, but Captain Preston, whom the judges decided *"did not give the order to fire on the civilians,"* was found not guilty. Judge Peter Oliver, brother of the Lieutenant Governor, said, *"this riot was perpetrated by villains, led by the tall man in the red cloak and white wig. This mystery man, who inspired the mob, is guilty in the sight of God of the five persons."* Bill Molineaux, thought to have been this agitating *"mystery man,"* had friends who said he was with them playing cards that night, and therefore could not have been at Dock Square to incite a riot.

There were no disturbances at Captain Preston's trial, but the Sons of Liberty crammed the courthouse when Privates Kilroy, Montgomery, Hategan, White, McCauley, Warren, Carroll, and Wemms were brought before the judges and jury. The day before the trial, the *Boston Gazette* headlined an anti-British article: *"Murder on the Fifth of March— Dogs greedily licking blood on King Street."* The paper also printed a pen and ink sketch by Paul Revere of five coffins, and Paul's engraving of the Massacre was hanging in many Boston living-rooms— John Adams' old pals certainly weren't helping his case. The courtroom was noisy, with shouts and occasional threats from the spectators. Bob Paine and Sam Quincy brought in many witnesses, as well as testimonies from 96 eye-witnesses, who swore the British soldiers fired without cause, and were not unduly provoked by the mob. Paine said there was *"a deliberate plot to attack citizens that evening,"* in retaliation for the ropeworkers' fight with Kilroy. Sam Quincy accused Kilroy of *"murder with malice,"* and said all the soldiers *"planned to attack and slaughter the inhabitants that night." "The soldiers started it,"* added Bob Paine, *"and you must unavoidably find Kilroy and Montgomery guilty of murder."* Josiah Quincy argued with his brother, *"the soldiers fired in self defense,"* and John Adams agreed— they had been attacked by *"a motley mob of saucy boys, negroes, mulattoes, Irish teagues, and outlandish Jack-Tars."* Even Patrick Carr, an Irish immigrant, who died eight days after he was shot in the belly, said *"the soldiers fired in self defense."* Eye-witnesses for the defense, like James Crawford and Archibald Wilson, testified, *"a number of people in the crowd had sticks in their hands, not common walking canes, but pretty large cudgels,"* and *"It is uncommon to go to a fire with bludgeons. . . Even the bells ringing that night were uncommon,"* added Wilson. The trial of the soldiers lasted 15 days. Only two of the eight accused, Kilroy and Montgomery, were found guilty — but of manslaughter, not murder.

The Sons of Liberty were furious with John Adams and Josiah Quincy, who were both active members of the Liberty Party, for winning the day for the British soldiers. The two guilty Redcoats were branded on the thumb as punishment, and although the hot-iron brought tears to their eyes, most New Englanders considered the punishment too lenient. Even John Hancock, the most conservative Liberty Party member shouted *"Satin, with his chosen hand has opened the sluices of New England's blood. . . . Dark and Designing knaves,"* John roared to a gathering crowd, *"murderers! parricides! How dare you tread upon the earth which has drunk the blood of slaughtered innocence, shed by your hands!"* John Adams quit the Liberty Party, and said he would never again be involved in American politics.

In a strange circumstance of timing, the British Parliament, under the insistance of Lord North the new Prime Minister, repealed the Townshend Acts, *"with the exception of the tax on tea,"* on March 5 th, 1770, the day of the Boston Massacre. When word of the repeal reached Boston weeks later, there was great rejoicing. The Sons of Liberty cooked a bull on Boston Common and had a banquet in celebration— they named the bull they baked and consumed, *"Skin and Bones Tommy,"* after Governor Hutchinson. John Hancock was voted Speaker of the House of Representatives and approved by Hutchinson, but John, thinking his battle with the British was over, like John Adams, quit the Liberty Party, and returned to the less rebellious Whigs — Sam Adams feared Hancock was such a conservative that he might become a Tory. Many New England families, like the Adams' and Quincys, were divided, some members being pro-British Tories, and others being Whigs or Liberty Party members. With the repeal of the Townshend Acts, *"excepting tea,"* people began leaving the Liberty Party in droves, some because they felt leaders Sam Adams and Joe Warren had instigated the Boston Massacre, and others because they thought the battle with the British government was over. Sam Adams was at a low ebb in his popularity. He accepted a job as a Boston constable and tax collector, and going from house to house with his little black collection bag, he somehow misplaced $7,000 pounds sterling. He was called before Town Meeting members to explain the loss, which he never could do satisfactorily — John Hancock had to make up the loss for him. When John Adams heard of Sam's dilemma, he commented, *"It's no wonder, for he lives like a grasshopper."*

Sam Adams and Joe Warren continued their uphill battle to stimulate complete independence from Mother England, with the help of trusty lieutenants like Bill Molineaux and Paul Revere. They initiated The Committees of Correspondence, *"to communicate and publish the rights of the Colonists and the violations of the British Parliament, to several Towns in New England."* Each Town then organized its own Committees of Correspondence, linking them all together in a communications network, which Governor Hutchinson complained, *"brought this Province from a state of peace, order and general contentment, into a state of contention, disorder and general disatisfaction."* Sam Adams wrote a series of letters which were circulated throughout New England and to other Colonies, through these Committees, keeping everyone abreast of all issues and any dastardly deeds, no matter how slight, committed by the British government in America. Ben Franklin made the mistake of sending Sam some letters written years before by Tom Hutchinson to a friend in England, which Ben asked Sam to keep secret, but they were *"so very unfavorable to the temper of the people in Massachusetts,"* Sam had them published. John Hancock was shocked at what Hutchinson had to say about him and other local leaders in these letters, and he rejoined the Liberty Party — John Adams soon followed suit. Bostonians were justly upset at Hutchinson's nasty letters about their prior conduct during the Stamp Riots, and the House of Representatives even tried to have Governor Hutchinson and his brother-in-law Lt. Governor Oliver, removed from office. In sending these *"secret"* letters to Sam, Parliament forced Ben Franklin to leave London, and he lost his job as Postmaster General. *"Ben Franklin is a poor politician,"* said Sam, but there was no doubt that Sam Adams was a good one, and a master propagandist.

Although few New Englanders worried about the three-cents tax on tea, Sam reminded them continuously that if Parliament was allowed to tax tea, no matter how little the tax, they would forever have the power to tax Americans in any way they pleased, on any item. He stressed a continuous boycott on buying English tea, which pleased the merchants, for they had been smuggling in Dutch tea without paying duty. Sam also reminded the citizens that the twelve British warships stationed in Boston Harbor, and the troops at Castle Island, were not here for their protection, but for *"the benefit of a greedy British Ministry."* New Englanders loved English tea, especially a type called Bohea, which most merchants refused to sell or import, causing Tories to complain that the boycott *"is a plot, a scandalous invasion of our tea-table priviledges, forcing us to drink that detestable and accursed liquor, rum."* As clever and farsighted as Sam Adams was, he couldn't have foreseen the explosive results of this little boycott on English tea, but in retrospect, one must wonder if he didn't realize all along what might happen, with a little extra patience and prodding on his part.

At secret meetings of *"the Long Room Club,"* Sam Adams and 14 other Liberty Party writers and strategists met periodically to pen articles for the Massachusetts Gazette, letters to the Committees of Correspondence, and features for their new radical publication, *"The Massachusetts Spy."* The magazine-like *"Spy"* was printed upstairs in the Union Oyster House, a restaurant that still stands in downtown Boston today, and carried articles that Tories and Englishmen considered treasonous. The publisher was Isaiah Thomas, who later became famous publishing *"Mother Goose"* and other children's books. He started setting type when he was six years old for a book titled *"Our Polly Is A Sad Slut,"* about a local prostitute. The youngest of the Long Room Club conspirators was teenager Thomas Melville, a graduate of Princeton, who was to become the grandfather of the author of *"Moby Dick."* Three others who submitted articles were the doctors, Joe Warren, Thomas Young and Ben Church. Doctor Young, who John Adams said *"talked too much,"* was an atheist and Doc Warren's professional rival. He, however, was a talented writer and submitted an effective treatise to the Massachusetts Spy and Boston Gazette on the harmful effects of drinking tea. *"It will induce hypochondria, melancholy and despair,"* wrote Doctor Young and, to be sure that American housewives wouldn't be tempted to drink tea, he added that *"it weakens the stomach lining."* Doc Warren did Tom Young one better, and wrote an article on tea, in which he reported that *"tea causes cancer."* Doctor Ben Church, *"a rogue"* wrote John Adams, *"who doesn't give a damn . . . . and supports a mistress,"* also wrote patriotic articles and gave fiery speeches on independence and the illegality of the tea tax. Church, although wealthy and owner of a mansion in Raynham, seemed always in need of money to support his womanizing. He, in fact, persuaded John Hancock, seemingly a pious man, to give up his girl friend of eight years and take a dock-side mistress, sharing her expenses with Ben Church. Hancock *"dismissed"* his old girl friend in a letter, and temporarily became a *"wild dandy,'* but soon met the stabilizing force in his life, Dolly Quincy, whom he later married. Doc Warren's effectiveness as a freedom fighter and writer temporarily waned in April of 1773, when his wife Elizabeth died. Eight days later, Paul Revere's wife *"Sary"* died after bearing Paul's eighth child. Paul soon remarried. His new wife Rachel provided him with eight more children — one was named Joseph Warren Revere, which indicates how much Paul revered his patriotic leader and family physician. Two other members of this secret, so-called literary society of American propagandists were Benjamin Edes and Moses Gill, publishers of the Boston Gazette. Their office was in an alley behind the Old State House, where the Long Room Club often met *"above the printing room."* Ben Burt, a 360-pound articulate silversmith and John Pulling, whom Tories called *"a Mohawk bully,"* were also members of this exclusive club.

Partly because of America's tea boycott and partly because of mismanagement, the British East India Company, which monopolized the tea industry out of England, was close to bankruptcy. The Company had a surplus of over 17 million pounds of tea sitting in warehouses in England, and Parliament allowed the Company to slash the price of tea to well below the cost of Dutch tea, but the tax on tea to America would remain. Four merchant ships, loaded with cargoes of tea, headed for Boston and six others headed to more southern ports in America, their Tory owners convinced that the low tea price would demolish the boycott. At Boston, on November 5, 1773, Guy Fawkes Day, there was a Town Meeting at Faneuil Hall, and a list of the tea consignees was announced to the near 1,000 people from Boston and surrounding towns who had gathered there. Three of the men named as consignees, who would make small fortunes on the tea shipments once they arrived in port, were Governor Hutchinson's two sons and his nephew — another was the wealthy Tory Richard Clarke, Lieutenant Governor Oliver's brother-in-law. *"Voted,"* shouted the Town Meeting moderator after a show of hands, *"that this body will oppose the vending of any tea sent by the East India Company to any part of this Continent, with our lives and fortunes."* There were three great cheers that rocked the hall. *"Voted,"* he shouted again, *"that Doctors Warren, Benjamin Church and Thomas Young, in committee, draft a resolution to be read to the tea agents, that they be at the Liberty Tree tomorrow at noon to pledge not to land or pay duties on tea. In case they do not appear, this body will esteem them enemies to their country; and will not fail to make them feel the weight of their resentment."*

A mob led by Molineaux went to Clarke's house in the middle of the night to deliver the ultimatum drafted by the three doctors. Clarke listened, but didn't respond, nor did he show up at the Liberty Tree next day. At 1:00 p.m. that day, a gang of some 200 Liberty Boys led by Warren and Molineaux tracked Clarke down to his warehouse at the foot of King Street. Clarke had some of his own bullyboys with him in his counting-house on the second floor. Molineaux shouted at him to *"promise you will not land the tea, but send it back."* *"I will have nothing to do with you,"* Clarke replied. With hoots and hollers, the two groups of bullyboys clashed on the stairway, but Molineaux called his men outside and had them surround the warehouse, where they held Clarke and his men captive inside for two hours, then they dispersed. Clarke and Hutchinson's nephew had letters slipped under their doors that evening, which read, *"this is the last warning you are ever to expect from the insulted, abused, and most indignant vindicators of violated liberty in the town of Boston."* Governor Hutchinson's Boston home was also visited, but he and his sons were at their vacation retreat in Milton, Massachusetts, some ten miles away.

On November 28th, the first tea-ship, **DARTMOUTH**, under command of Captain Jim Rotch, arrived in Boston, and the consignees wanted to store his cargo of 114 chests of tea in a warehouse, but the Boston Town Fathers demanded that the tea be returned to England. Three days later, the **BEAVER**, under Captain Coffin arrived with more tea, and then ten days later, the **ELEANOR** pulled into port, but the tea-ship **WILLIAM** didn't make it. Carrying 58 heavy chests of tea, she wrecked off Cape Cod. The three ship captains were willing to return the tea to England as the people wanted, but the Governor, still vacationing in Milton, sent a letter stating that by law, he could not allow the vessels to leave Boston until they disposed of their cargoes. At Castle Island, the new British troop commander, Colonel Alexander Leslie, was ordered to have his artillery and the men-of-war in the outer harbor, fire on any tea-ship that attempted to leave port with cargo. The captains of the tea-ships were stuck between a rock and a hardplace — they couldn't leave and they couldn't stay. As usual, Sam Adams came up with a brilliant idea to solve the impasse.

"A general muster," writes John Andrews, *"was assembled from this and all the neighboring towns, to the number of five or six thousand people,"* on the Thursday morning of December 16, 1773. Faneuil Hall was not big enough to hold them all, so the meeting was moved to the Old South Church. The first and only order of business that day was what to do with the 348 chests of tea sitting in the three vessels tied to Griffen's Wharf. Famous artist John Singleton Copley, who had just finished two portraits of John Hancock and Sam Adams, paid for by John to hang in his sitting room, begged the crowd that the tea be allowed storage in the warehouse. Copley was consignee Richard Clarke's son-in-law — the crowd roared *"No!"* Captain Rotch was sent off to Milton in one last attempt to persuade the Governor to release the vessels so that they might return to England with the tea. While he was gone, Josiah Quincy entertained the crowd with a patriotic speech. *"I see the clouds which now rise thick and fast upon our horizon. The thunder rolls and the lightning plays, and to that God who rides the whirlwind and directs the storm, I commit my country. . . ."* Quincy went on for two hours, but many there didn't need stimulating speeches, they already knew what the end of the day would bring. Revere and his fellow spies were watching the ships, and had already alerted other seaports not to allow tea in. Posters were plastered everywhere: *"Friends! Brethren! Countrymen!"* they read, *"that worst plague, the detested tea shipped for this port is now arrived in the Harbour. The hour of destruction stares you in the face. . . ."*

"When Captain Rotch returned from Milton," writes John Andrews, who was sitting in his home nearby, *"the candles were light in the*

houses. " The Governor had told Rotch that *"It is not in my power to give clearance, without duties being first paid,"* and that, *"the tea would be unloaded on schedule."* George Hewes was outside the Old South Meeting House, but it was so packed, he couldn't get in to find out what was going on. He finally climbed a tree and squeezed in through a window. Hancock was at the podium. *"The matter must be decided before twelve o'clock this night,"* John was saying. Then Sam Adams interrupted: *"This meeting can do nothing more to save this country."* Apparently this statement from Adams was a signal, for there was a *"war-whoop"* from a man disguised as an Indian at the rear of the hall, and his cry was echoed by others dressed like Indians from outside in nearby alleys. *"Let every man do what is right in his own eyes,"* shouted Hancock over the war-whoops. *"There was such prodigious shouts from the Meeting House,"* said John Andrews, *"that induced me, while drinking my tea at home, to go out and know the cause of it. . . There was another general shout, out doors and in, and three cheers. What with that, and the consequent noise of breaking up of the meeting, you'd thought that the inhabitants of the infernal regions had broken loose. For my part, I went contentedly home and finished my tea. . ."*

George Hewes ran home, and with soot from his fireplace and boot-black, he rubbed it onto his hands and face. He then tied a goose-feather from a pillow to his head, and wrapped himself in a blanket. His wife was upset— where was he going dressed up like that? Are you drunk? George smiled, but didn't answer— out the door he went, running to catch up with the others who were marching two-by-two to Griffen's Wharf. There were many in Indian costumes whom Hewes recognized, even though their faces were smeared with paint, soot, and grease. He spotted John Hancock, *"for he still wore ruffles,"* and young Melville by his baby face. He sauntered up to Melville and smiling said, *"Me know you!"*. *"I think Boston Harbor is a teapot tonight,"* replied Melville. *"Many were armed with hatchets, axes, and pistols,"* said Hewes, who was sorry he had forgotten to bring along his cobbler's hammer. In all, there were about 200 Indians, and they were divided into three groups, one for each tea-ship. *"As soon as we were on board,"* says Hewes, *"Lendall Pitt, my commander, appointed me the boatswain, and ordered me to go to the captain and demand of him the keys to the hatches and a dozen candles. I made the demand accordingly, and the captain promptly complied, but requested me to do no damage to the ship and rigging. We then opened the hatches and took out all the chests of tea. First we cut and split the chests to thoroughly expose them to the water, and thus broken, we threw overboard every tea chest to be found in the ship; while those in the other ships were disposing of the tea in the same way, at the same time, it being about three hours from the time we went on board. We were surrounded by British armed ships, but no attempt was made to resist us. . ."* One Indian, John Crane, accidentally fell into the hold of the BEAVER while hoisting up tea, and he was left there for dead, but he revived two hours later.

One rule that was passed along from Indian to Indian as they unloaded the tea, was that no one was to take even a pinch of tea for themselves, but one or two were tempted and they paid dearly for it. An Irish-Indian named Conner, *"had ript up the lining of his coat under the arms, and had nearly filled 'em with tea, but being detected was handled pretty roughly. The Indians not only stripped him of his clothes, but gave him a coat of mud, with a severe beating into the bargain."* There were twelve and thirteen year old boys at the Tea Party too, most of them apprentice boys who had snuck out of their shops without their masters knowing. Peter Slater, whose Tory master locked him up in his room when he tried to join the Indians, succeeded in escaping by tying his bedding together and slipping out a second-story window. One of the Indians gave him and some other boys the job of stomping into the mud any tea that collected on the mud-flats near the ships. There were such piles of tea in the mud that the boys couldn't stomp it all down. When the men completed their dumping at about 9:30 p.m., many of the boys remained at the tea ships and didn't finish their chore until about 11:00 p.m. Young Henry Purkitt got home after Midnight and stumbled into bed exhausted. In the morning, his mother found mounds of tea from his discarded clothes all over his bedroom. She scooped it up in a bottle, and the Purkitt family retains some of the tea from the Tea Party to this day.

Sam Adams had planned the Tea Party in style, even with a fife and drum band there to meet the Indians on the dock when they had finished with their work. As the Indians marched away, British Admiral Montagu, who was staying with friends near the wharf, pushed open his window shutters. *"You'll have to pay the fiddler yet,"* he shouted at George Hewes, Lendall Pitts and the others as they passed by. *"You have had a fine pleasant evening for your Indian caper, haven't you?"* *"Come out here,"* Pitts shouted back, *"and we'll settle the bill in two minutes."* The Admiral pulled the shutters and slammed his window shut. George, like a real Indian, tried to sneak quietly into his house, but his wife was waiting for him. She demanded an explanation, so Hewes told her the whole story. She seemed to grow angrier as Hewes explained, and when he finished she stomped off to bed, *"madder than a wet hen,"* says Hewes, *"that I didn't bring her home any tea."*

IV
ALL THE KING'S MEN

The British Prime Minister, Lord North, ordered the port of Boston closed to all merchant shipping, in or out, until Bostonians paid for the 10,000 pounds-sterling worth of tea destroyed at the Tea Party. Salem was designated as the new port of entry for British merchants trading in Massachusetts. This was economic death for the sailors, dockworkers and merchants of Boston. The King also ordered General Gage to send more troops to the rebellious colony, and that he should become the military Governor of Massachusetts — that was the bad news. The good news was that Governor Tom Hutchinson was called to England by the King's Ministers, never to return to Boston, and Lieutenant Governor Oliver dropped dead. As Oliver was lowered into his grave, many Liberty Boys stood on the outskirts of the cemetery, hooting and hollering, but John Hancock was at graveside as a legitimate mourner. When Hutchinson's son Elisha, the East India Company tea agent, returned to Boston in January, 1774, after his extended vacation, he was chased out of town by the Liberty Boys in the middle of a blizzard, forced to leave all his possessions behind.

A few nights later George Hewes was walking home through Boston Common. It was the chilly, snowy evening of January 25, 1774. On the Common path, he spied a boy being beaten by a man with a walking stick. George rushed to the boy's aid and grabbed the stick from the angry man. The boy was crying, and said he was only packing firewood onto his sled when the man accosted him. *"The sled is in the path, blocking my way,"* growled the man, who George recognized as Johnny Malcolm, an eccentric Tory who worked at the British customs office. Malcolm, however, at first thought Hewes was a little boy, and he told him to leave or he would be flogged as well. Malcolm then kicked the boy's sled over, grabbed his stick from George, and whacked George as hard as he could over the head, cracking his skull. George fell unconscious into the snow and Malcolm ran off. The boy ran to Doctor Warren's house for help. Hewes regained consciousness as two men carried him to the doctor's house. *"You're lucky you have such a thick skull,"* said Doc Warren as he stitched and bandaged him up. *"Most men would have died from the blow."* Warren called for the sheriff, and he, with George and some of Warren's Liberty Boys went to Malcolm's house. Malcolm barricaded his doors and wouldn't let the sheriff in, then he opened a second story window and aimed a pistol at the crowd that was gathering outside. *"I'll shoot any Yankee that tries to come in,"* he shouted, and then he proceeded to spit on everyone below. A neighbor ran home for a ladder, and it was put up to the window. Malcolm now had an axe in one hand and a sword in the other, which he waved at the men who started climbing the ladder. As they, one by one, forced themselves into Malcolm's house through the window, fending off his blows, the sheriff decided to leave. Malcolm was disarmed after one intruder was sliced by Malcolm's sword, and then they forced him out the window and down the ladder to the waiting arms of the Liberty Boys.

Malcolm was squeezed into a little sled and driven to the nearby wharf, feeling an occasional fist if he dared to move an arm or a leg or say anything. At the wharf, some twenty men stripped him to the waist and painted him with hot tar. Two torn feather pillows were thrown into his face and the feathers stuck to the tar. By this time, over 1,000 spectators had gathered to watch and shout their approval. George, who had now become just another bystander, felt sorry for Malcolm, *"who looked like a half-plucked chicken."* George was amazed that his cracked skull had caused such a commotion. Malcolm, shivering from cold and fear, was then driven through the streets of Boston in the little sled for four hours, with occasional stops at taverns and at various trees, where the crowd threatened to hang him. There was a long delay at the Liberty Tree, where pots of hot tea were prepared and forced down Malcolm's throat. In between burning gulps, he was made to make up appropriate toasts to various members of the Royal Family and Parliament. *"Drink to their health,"* the crowd roared as the tea was forced down his gullet — three quarts of tea in all, and Malcolm threw up three times. He was continuously flogged with sticks along the way until bits of his frozen flesh flaked to the ground — then the bruised and half frozen victim was driven back home.

With bits of tar still hanging from his flesh, and a package of feathers under his arm *"to show the King,"* Johnny Malcolm returned to his native England, where, for all his troubles, he received a pension and was allowed to retire from his hazardous occupation as customs official. John Adams said that *"the tarring and feathering of Malcolm was the luckiest event in his entire miserable life."* Another of the Sons of Liberty, probably Sam Adams, placed a statement in the Boston Gazette: *"Brethern and Fellow Citizens,"* it read, *"This is to certify that the modern punishment lately inflicted on the ignoble John Malcolm was not done by Our Order. We reserve that method for bringing villains of greater consequence to a sense of guilt and infamy"* — and it was signed, *"Joyce Junior, Chairman of the Committee of Tarring and Feathering."* Poor George Hewes was getting a complex, for he always seemed to be at the right place at the wrong time, or the wrong place at the right time — the Revolution seemed to be revolving around him.

General Thomas Gage was back in Boston Town again on May 13, 1774. Part of Colonel Leslie's 64th Regiment was brought in from Castle Island at Gage's arrival and were quartered in the North End of town. The King's own Regiment, the Royal Irish, and the 43rd Regiment arrived in Boston on June 1st. The Fifth and 38th Regiments arrived later. The Royal Welch Fusilliers and the Royal Artillery were shipped up from New York and camped on Boston Common. Now, besides depression and unemployment, restless, quarrelsome Redcoats once again walked the streets of Boston, further harrassing the populace. Before the summer was over, General Gage had eleven regiments stationed in Boston — over 5,000 Redcoats, living in tents, makeshift barracks, and in the homes of distressed Bostonians. Their presence, especially on Boston Common, so upset Bill Molineaux, who lived near the Common, that he dropped dead of a heart-attack. One Boston Tory said that he died from *"inflammation of the bowels."* Other Liberty Party leaders underwent grave hardships too, with the closing of the port and the advent of British troops. Slave-trader John Rowe's daughter fell in love with a British soldier and wanted to marry him, which almost drove Rowe mad with grief. John Hancock's fiancée Dorothy Quincy had the hots for Major-General Lord Percy, commander of the Fifth Regiment, which camped in front of John's mansion on the Common and John was wildly jealous. Mary Dill Thomas, wife of publisher Isiah Thomas, was seeing a bevy of British officers on the sly, and Isiah had to drag her off to Worcester to temper her sex drive. Many other wives, daughters, and sweethearts were becoming enchanted with this glut of uniformed men that suddenly appeared on the scene, causing duels, fist fights and many other disturbances in Boston Town.

Only three weeks after he arrived in Boston, General Gage announced that the General Court would no longer sit in Boston, but would meet at Salem, which the Crown now considered to be the Capitol of Massachusetts. Hancock, Adams, and the other legislators squawked, but General Gage assured them that *"it is the King's particular command to meet at Salem."* This meeting that lasted from June 7th to June 17th, didn't go well for the General. His first meeting with the Massachusetts Legislature, which included Hancock, Warren, and the Adams', was his last. He refused to convene the legislature again, but they met anyway, again at Salem on October 5th, and formed their own new Provincial Congress to govern Massachusetts. General Gage's secretary Thomas Flucker arrived at the Salem Court House to read General Gage's proclamation dissolving the General Court, but

Hancock and the others wouldn't let Flucker in the door. He read the General's order on the front steps, but nobody listened. Inside, the legislature adopted Joe Warren's suggestion for an American *"Committee of Safety,"* establishing rules, regulations, communications, training of minutemen, secret supply depots, and the manufacture of weapons *"for public safety in New England during this crisis."* They also agreed to Warren's demand that *"New England merchants not sell British goods, and that anyone who didn't agree was to be branded a traitor."* Warren wrote to Sam Adams in Salem, *"Vigilance, activity and patience are necessary at this time, but the mistress we court is Liberty, and it is better to die than not to obtain her."*

The new independent Massachusetts Congress sent Josiah Quincy to England from Salem to attempt a compromise with Parliament and the King's Ministers, but he was unsuccessful, and Josiah died of his tubercular cough on his way back to New England. Sam Adams, with cousin John, Tom Cushing, Jim Bowdoin, and Robert Treat Paine, were elected as delegates by the new Provincial Congress to meet with 52 delegates of the other Colonies at Philadelphia who were also upset about the British occupation of Boston. Traveling the 350 miles to Philadelphia was considered a great chore for Sam Adams, for he would have to learn how to ride a horse first, yet in the first year after the Tea Party, Warren had Paul Revere ride to Philly four times with various resolves to submit to the new Congress. Paul never complained, but Sam, after only an hour on a horse, protested *"I have a sore-arse."* For his journey South, Sam's neighbors chipped in and bought him a new suit, *"to keep his shanks covered,"* one neighbor said, but they really did it so that their slovenly representative would look presentable to other members of Congress. Arch enemies John Adams and Bob Paine rode much of the way to Philadelphia together, and surprisingly found that they got along quite well. Upon arrival John wrote, *"Boston is but a village compared to Philadelphia, but our language is better, our taste is better, our persons are handsomer. . ."*

The Congressional delegates at Philadelphia also accepted Joe Warren's resolves to boycott all British products and establish Committees of Safety, which basically prepared America for war. One Boston Tory said that these Congressmen *"accepted the resolves only because they had just drunk thirty-two bumpers of Madeira wine."* The date set to embargo all British goods in America was December 1, 1774. Joe Warren and Sam Adams had sparked what England's Lord Dartmouth called, *"plainly a state of rebellion."* In a letter to the King, the Congressmen pledged their loyalty, but listed their many complaints, and after two months of discussions and passed resolves they adjourned, agreeing to meet again in Philadelphia in May, 1775, not realizing, of course, what was to happen to change their lives and the world, only three weeks before their planned meeting.

In the meantime, General Gage had his troops march and drill on Boston Common every day, with occasional marches out into the countryside, *"to keep my men active and healthy,"* he said. These tromps through suburbia unnerved the country folks, and the Sons of Liberty feared that the troops were after their precious ammunition, which was stored in powder-houses in almost every village and New England town. *"Wherever our armies march,"* wrote British Colonel Charles Stuart, *"every species of barbarity has been executed. We planted an irrecoverable hatred wherever we went, which neither time nor measures will be able to eradicate."* When Gage did confiscate a supply of colonial ammunition and cannons from the Charlestown powder-house secretly at Dawn on September 1, 1774, the countryside was alerted and up-in-arms. Hundreds of angry men greeted Redcoats on the road, but it was after they had moved the powder and four brass cannons from the Charlestown powder-house to a barn in Boston. Joe Warren went to Charlestown and then Cambridge to calm the angry Minutemen who congregated there, ready to kill Redcoats. Rumor was that the troops had not only confiscated the ammunition supply at Charlestown, but had killed six citizens. Even Minutemen as far away as Connecticut had heard the rumor and were ready to march on Boston. Warren's Committees of Safety were working well, almost too well, and even General Gage wrote to England that he was *"horrified that so many had risen up against our troops,"* and he asked that more soldiers be sent to Boston. This incident caused Gage to begin construction of another fort at Boston Neck, and prompted the Sons of Liberty to move their meager supplies of arms and ammunition to new secret locations.

Warren and Revere also beefed-up their spy-ring, assigning Liberty Boys to watch the movements of every British regiment in town, and whenever possible to join British officers in conversation at local taverns. Revere, however, was plagued by the worry *"that our meetings are discovered. . . . We find that all our transactions are communicated to General Gage. . . . It is common opinion that there is a traitor in the Provincial Congress, and that Gage is possessed of all our secrets."* Besides *"the traitor"* who posed as a loyal Son of Liberty, Gage had other British spies, who wandered the countryside in civilian clothes, gathering information on activities of militiamen, Liberty Party leaders, and the whereabouts of ammunition and weapon supplies. Most of

Gage's spies considered the New England militiamen who drilled once a month on Saturdays at the various village greens, *"not soldiers but bumpkins."* Only officers of the militia companies wore uniforms, whereas the rest of the men wore *"their Sunday-best suits,"* and they were considered amateurs by the British when it came to marching and drilling — many militiamen didn't even carry muskets at training. *"These training days are occasion for general frolic,"* Gage was informed, but the General was no fool, for he had served with the Americans during the French and Indian War, and was aware of their ability as marksmen. The British also weren't aware of the difference between militiamen and Minutemen, the latter being Sons of Liberty volunteers, ready to fight on a minute's notice by the Committee of Safety.

One of Gage's spies, Private John Howe, while snooping around Lexington wearing civilian clothes, stopped to talk to an old man who was outside his house cleaning his musket. *"I asked the old man what he was going to kill,"* Howe reported to General Gage, *"as he was so old I should not think he could take sight at any game. He said there was a flock of Redcoats at Boston. I asked him how he expected to fight. He said open field fighting, or any other way to kill them Redcoats."* Private Howe also reported that after returning to Boston from a spying mission in Worcester, he was called before Colonel Smith, General Gage, and a few other superior officers, who, Howe said, *"had all been taking their bumpers* (drinking liquor) *rather freely."* General Gage asked Howe, how many soldiers he thought it might take to capture Worcester's supply of arms and ammunition. *"Over ten-thousand regular infantry and a train of artillery,"* the young spy replied, *"but not one of them would get back alive."* The officers laughed and scoffed at Howe, but the General said, *"Your judgement is very good for a beardless lad of twenty-two."* *"Concord however,"* Howe informed Gage and the others, *"would be an easy take,"* for he had discovered where the Minutemen had hidden all their supplies at Concord.

In January, 1775, General Gage was forced to send a sloop filled with Redcoats to Marshfield, to protect the Tories living there, who were being forced out of town by a wild mob of Liberty Boys, and less than a month before, as Gage planned to move troops to the lightly guarded British fort at Portsmouth, New Hampshire, it was taken over by Minutemen, and some 100 barrels of gunpowder were confiscated. Paul Revere had warned John Sullivan, New Hampshire's leader of the Committee of Safety, that Gage intended to protect the fort with a regiment of troops, so Sullivan and some 200 men raided the fort before the reinforcements came, without hurting the six soldiers who then guarded the gunpowder. The powder was taken away by boats and hidden under the pulpit at the Durham meeting-house. Gage's anticipated troop movement to New Hampshire was innocently revealed to Boston bookstore owner Henry Knox by Gage's secretary, Thomas Flucker, who was Knox's father-in-law, and passed on to Joe Warren. Warren, at the same time he sent Revere to Portsmouth, sent another messenger to the Committee of Safety at Newport, Rhode Island, telling them that his spies had discovered that Gage intended to send 300 Redcoats there as well.

General Gage, not to be outwitted in this spy intrigue, was aware that Paul Revere was Warren's lieutenant, and that Paul had received a pass from the British to leave Boston for New Hampshire on the day before Sullivan and his men robbed Fort William And Mary of the gunpowder. One of the General's spies, keeping an eye on discontents at Salem, where local merchants were smuggling blackmarket goods into Boston in carts aptly called *"Lord North Coasters,"* discovered that these same Salemites were hiding illegal cannons in the fields on the outskirts of town. Instead of moving out troops from Boston, Gage called on Colonel Leslie at Castle Island to secretly sail with 300 of his troops to Marblehead, *"and thence march to Salem to confiscate these cannons."* Two days before Leslie and his men were ready to embark on their secret mission, the versatile Paul Revere was discovered by the British in a rowboat, *"fishing"* off Castle Island. He was delayed for two days at the Castle Island Fort, while Leslie and his men sailed off at Midnight, February 25th, to Marblehead in hopes of surprising the residents of Salem. Leslie's regiment hid in the hold of the ship until Sunday noon, when the Colonel knew everyone would be at church, but when the soldiers landed at Marblehead, John Pedrick, Paul Revere's North Shore counterpart, saddled his horse and rode the six miles from Marblehead to Salem, where he pounded on all the church doors, shouting, *"The British are coming!"* By the time the Redcoats arrived at the North Bridge, which was conveniently a draw-bridge— the draw was up, barring further progress for the Redcoats into North Salem, where the cannons were hidden. Crowds gathered on both sides of the bridge spewing insults and curses at the British soldiers, who could march no further. Leslie demanded that the bridge-leaf be lowered, as Captain John Felt, nudging the Colonel with his elbow, threatened to push him into the icy river if he didn't march back to Marblehead. *"I'll cross this river if it takes 'til Autumn,"* shouted Leslie. *"I don't think nobody would mind that,"* laughed Felt. Felt finally agreed to have the bridge-leaf lowered if Leslie would march across, then turn around and march back to his ship. Leslie, surprisingly agreed. The only man hurt during the bridge impasse was a black man named Joe Whicher, who was bayoneted as he tried to sink a boat that was at the river's edge. The slight wound became his medal of honor in Salem Town. The incident became known as *"Leslie's Retreat,"* and once back in Boston, General Gage shipped Colonel Leslie back home to Scotland in disgrace. *"The Americans have hoisted their standard of liberty at Salem,"* wrote the editor of England's *"Gentleman's Magazine,"* *"and there is little doubt that the next news will be an account of a bloody engagement between the two armies."* King George III came before Parliament and announced, *"Massachusetts is in a state of Rebellion."* The King wasn't insane, as insinuated, he was just slow.

Since the British troops and the Tory loyalists of Boston had a gala celebration with banquets and fireworks on January 18, 1775, in honor of the Queen's birthday, Adams and Warren decided to do them one better on March 5th, commemorating the Boston Massacre. *"It is good politics,"* said Sam Adams, *"to put and keep the enemy in the wrong."* Parades, speeches, fireworks, banquets and bonfires were planned for that day and night, and a great crowd gathered at the Old South Church and Meeting House that morning, where Joe Warren was to make a keynote speech. Sam Adams, in fact, invited General Gage and all the British officers in Town to come and hear Warren, and Sam reserved front row seats in the hall for them *"to be sure they hear every word."* Paul Revere, a bit unnerved after his lock-up at Castle Island, was further unsettled when he overheard British officers say that there was a plan afoot to assassinate Joe Warren as he gave his speech at the Old South Meeting House. The plan, as Paul understood it, was that a British Lieutenant would throw an egg at Warren as he stood at the podium. That was the signal for two other officers to shoot Warren at close range.

When Warren appeared at the Meeting House on the morning of March 5th, well aware of the assassination plot, it was so crowded that he couldn't get in the front door, and he was forced to climb in a rear window. Although General Gage decided not to attend, the front row was filled with stern-faced British officers of all the regiments but the Forty-Third. They were marching with their troops in the countryside. Gage feared that the Boston ceremonies might be another of Sam Adams' clever ploys, and that Minutemen from surrounding towns might attack Boston while his officers were gathered under Sam's roof. Sam, as the moderator, introduced Warren as the man *"who shall speak on the bloody massacre."* As some of the British officers heckled, Warren began, *"Take heed ye orphan babes, lest whilst your straining eyes are fixed upon the ghostly corpse, your feet slide on the stones bespattered with your father's brains. . . . "* The British officers squirmed in their seats, and sitting behind them, the Liberty Boys leaned forward, lips and fists clenched. *"After such a tragedy, "* Warren continued, *"one would not have expected to see the British Army in Boston again. . . . . "* Cheers from the rear and booes from the front reverberated off the walls. *"We shall fight until tyranny is defeated, "* Warren shouted. Liberty Boys were on their feet applauding, the British officers were shouting and hissing, stomping the floor with their swagger-sticks. Warren expected the egg to be thrown any minute, and the window behind the podium was open so he could quickly leap out when he saw the egg coming. Just as he completed his speech, there came the roll of drums and the tramp of marching feet outside the church — the 43rd Regiment, back from its trek in the country, was blocking the front door. *"Fire!"* a British officer in the front row of the meeting-house shouted, *"and all-hell broke loose. "*

Some Liberty Boys jumped out the windows, women were screaming, British officers, with backs turned to the podium, waved their swagger-sticks, jeering as citizens fled out the door and through the ranks of the 43rd Regiment standing at attention outside. Warren and Adams were quickly prodded out a back window by friends as most of the crowd fled in panic. Others shouted and waved their fists at the soldiers. General Gage immediately called out all his troops, and announced the cancellation of further activities and festivities planned for the afternoon and evening. Joe Warren and Sam Adams were escorted back to Warren's house, which was now the secret headquarters for the Liberty Party. Rumor around town was that Gage planned to arrest them and John Hancock for treason. Paul Revere thought it best that they be hustled out of town. Warren, again the stabilizing force, calmed everyone and begged them not to act or react on rumors. *"But what of the egg, "* he asked Revere, *"it never came. "* Revere then explained that the plot to kill Warren had been real, but was upset when the lieutenant carrying the egg fell outside the Meeting House, *"and broke his knee-cap, as well as the egg. "*

A few nights later, John Hancock's house was attacked by Redcoats. They tore up his fencing and broke windows, then shouted for him to show himself, which he did. *"Go home, or I'll report you to your superior officers, "* he told them, realizing that it was probably their officers who sent them to harrass him. They cursed him, broke a few more windows and left. The following day at Boston Neck, where official executions took place, as Warren rode to see a sick patient, three British officers on horseback blocked his way. *"You may pass Warren, "* one scoffed as they allowed Warren to gallop by, *"for you soon will be back here to hang on these gallows. "* Warren cringed at the remark, turned his horse around and faced the officers. *"Which of you said that?"* Warren demanded with fire in his eyes, but none of the three answered. It was known about town that the doctor had a fierce temper and always carried two pistols under his coat. *"I demand to know who is the coward who made that statement,"* Warren shouted into their faces, which now matched their scarlet uniforms. He still didn't get an answer, so he rode on to his doctor duties, fuming — it was quite apparent to Warren, as it was to General Gage, that things were getting hot — everyone in Massachusetts had short fuses, and a great explosion was due. The calm, cool and collected Joe Warren was getting tense and nervous, but was determined to keep his Rebels alert and ready for action. Yet, in rare and quiet moments, he felt as vulnerable as the cracked egg that failed as the signal to assassinate him — he considered himself like the character in one of Isiah Thomas' nursery-rhymes — *"Humpty-Dumpty sat on a wall, Humpty-Dumpty had a great fall, but all the King's horses and all the King's men, couldn't put Humpty-Dumpty back together again. "*

The Battle of Lexington by noted illustrator Howard Pyle.

V
HELL TO PAY TOMORROW

Paul Revere heard from three of his spies prior to April 14th that the British troops were planning to march into the country to confiscate weapons and ammunition hidden by the Sons of Liberty. Revere and Warren agreed that their destination would probably be Concord where the Committee of Safety had stored a large quantity of gunpowder, musketballs, and a few precious cannons. Revere rode to Concord on the 14th to warn the Minutemen that the British might be heading their way soon in an attempt to destroy these stores. A Boston stableboy, named John Ballard, confirmed Revere's fears on the afternoon of April 18th. While combing a British officer's horse, he overheard the officer's groom say, *"There will be hell to pay tomorrow!"* Young Ballard snuck away from his duties, but afraid to go directly to Revere's house or shop, he told another Liberty Boy he met on Anne Street to pass the information on to Paul — *"The British are preparing to strike tomorrow."* Upon receiving this information, Revere went directly to Warren's house. Warren concluded that the British might not be after the Concord supply depot, but probably were going after Sam Adams and John Hancock who were meeting with other members of the Provincial Congress near Concord at Menotomy (Arlington) on that very day.

Actually, General Gage's plan was to capture Adams and Hancock and to destroy the ammunition supply depot at Concord as well. After Colonel Leslie's Retreat at Salem, Gage had received a letter from the King's Ministers, *"to test the people to see if they are willing to fight. . . . If there is going to be a war,"* wrote Lord Dartmouth, *"let it be brought on immediately, before the Colonials can develop an Army."* On Tuesday the 18th, the General ordered his commanders to prepare the troops to march that evening, but he told only Lord Percy, commander of the Fifth Regiment, that their destination was Concord. The only other person General Gage told that the troops were going to secretly sneak out of Boston that night and march to Concord, was his wife Margaret. She was American, not English, and when the General realized later that the Yankee Rebels were well informed about his supposedly secret maneuver, he suspected that his wife might have told them.

When the troops began to move at 9 p.m. from the Boston Common to rowboats on the banks of the Charles River, Warren dispatched Billy Dawes, *"a long-nosed jester,"* who was one of his corps of couriers, to alert the Minutemen at Roxbury, Brighton and Cambridge, and then Dawes was to join Revere in Lexington. Revere left Warren's house at

10 p.m. on the night of April 18th. His mission was to warn Hancock and Adams, who were staying at Reverend Clark's Parsonage in Lexington, that the British were after them. Paul was also to alert all the Minutemen commanders along the way, at Medford, Menotomy, Lexington and then Concord, some 20 miles of riding in all. He had already set up a signal system with Bob Newman, the sexton of the North Church, to hang one or two lanterns in the belfry — *"one if by land and two if by sea,"* to alert Charlestown's Minuteman commander, Colonel Conant, which way the British were disembarking out of Boston, by foot or by boat. For sending that signal, Newman was arrested and jailed the next day. While the British troops were being rowed across the river to Lechmere Point, Cambridge, Paul Revere was being rowed across the river to Charlestown by Tom Richardson and Joshua Bentley. Paul was delayed however, for he had forgotten his spurs. His dog had followed him to the rowboat, so he tied a note to the dog's collar and ordered her to go home. Reading the note, Paul's wife attached the spurs to the dog's collar and sent her scurrying back to Paul with the equipment he needed to make his famous ride. At Charlestown, after having to row around the anchored British warship **SOMERSET**, Paul borrowed Deacon John Larkin's fastest horse *"Meg,"* and headed for Charlestown Neck, a narrow peninsula of saltmarsh that connected Charlestown with the mainland. There he met *"two British officers on horseback. One tried to get ahead of me, "* Paul later reported, *"and the other tried to take me. I turned my horse short about and rode at full gallop for Mistick Road, easily out distancing the British. . . . I alarmed almost every house till I got to Lexington. "*

Paul banged on the door of Clark's Parsonage at Midnight, shouting to Hancock and Adams to let him in. Surprisingly, Hancock's fat Aunt Lydia and Dolly Quincy were there, in their nightgowns. Old squarejawed Deacon Jonas Clark, led Paul into the kitchen where Adams and Hancock sat, only recently arrived themselves from a Committee of Safety meeting at Weatherby's Black Horse Tavern in Menotomy. *"It's not just a British patrol that's after you, "* Paul breathlessly informed them, *"but over one-thousand regulars are on the march. "* Hancock immediately called to his Dolly to get him *"my sword and gun "* — he wanted to stand with the Minutemen to face the British Army on Lexington Green, which was but a stones-throw away from the parsonage. *"Foolishness, "* stammered Sam Adams, *"that is not our business. "* He then reminded John that they were to start for Philadelphia for the May meeting of Congress and, that if he were captured or dead, who would pay all the bills for needed supplies and weapons? Billy Dawes arrived at Clark's, and he and Revere ate at the kitchen table as Sam and John sat there and argued, while John cleaned his pistol and sword in preparation for the inevitable fight. Dolly Quincy, whom Sam said had *"laughing eyes and a nice little figure,"* also tried to persuade John not to join the Lexington Minutemen, who were at that moment meeting up the road at Buckman's Tavern.

By one a. m., Revere and Dawes were on the road again, heading for Concord some five miles away, to warn the Minutemen that the British were on the road coming to confiscate their ammunition and weapons. On their way out of Lexington they met Doctor Sam Prescott, another member of the Liberty Party, who was going home from a date with Miss Millikan. As the doctor rode along with them, Revere told him what was going on. Only a mile up the road, six British officers on horseback dashed onto the road from the bushes, their pistols drawn, confronting Paul, Billy and Sam Prescott. *"Damn you stop!"* shouted one, *"for if you advance an inch further, you are dead men."* Prescott immediately whipped his horse around, jumped over a nearby stonewall and made his escape into the woods and on to Concord to alert the Minutemen. Revere was about to try the same, *"but the officers seized my bridle, put their pistols to my breast and ordered me to dismount, which I did."* While Revere was being held captive, Dawes galloped on, with two British officers in hasty pursuit of him. He rode up a drive and stopped so quickly in front of a farmhouse that his pocketwatch jumped out of his pants pocket and landed on the ground. *"Hello Boys!"* he shouted towards the house, *"I've got two of them here, comin' up behind me."* The British, obviously thinking that Dawes had led them into a trap of armed Minutemen, reined their horses and sped away. The farmhouse, in fact, was empty, and Dawes, chuckling to himself, rode on. He came back for his watch later.

Meanwhile, Paul was telling his captors that he was Paul Revere, *"which caused some of them to abuse me much,"* and he also told them that, *"I have alarmed the countryside."* They called him *"a damned Rebel"* and threatened to *"blow my brains out,"* but then gun-fire was heard coming from Lexington. *"What was that shot for?"* British Major Edward Mitchell asked Revere. *"To alarm the country,"* replied Revere. Then came the sound of more gun-fire, which caused the British to gallop off, taking Revere's horse with them, leaving Paul alone on the road. He ducked into the bushes and stumbled a mile through woods and fields back to Clark's house. When he arrived back at Clark's kitchen, Hancock and Adams were still arguing, John Hancock determined *"to fight with the men who were now collecting on the green."* Dolly Quincy was so upset with John that she insisted Aunt

Lydia take her back to Boston. John said *"No"* — she was not to return to Boston. *"I am not under your control yet,"* shouted Dolly, *"and I shall go to my father tomorrow."* To add to the confusion, Hancock insisted that if he were to leave Lexington or not, he must have his heavy trunk containing his wardrobe for Philadelphia and some documents that certainly would bring Sam and him to the gallows if discovered by the British. The trunk was upstairs at Buckman's Tavern — *"would Paul help his clerk Mister Lowell carry the trunk to him,"* John wondered? Sam Adams was upset — he wanted to get out of Lexington quickly, so he constantly prodded John and purposely embarrassed him about all the baggage he carried with him as they traveled from place to place. Sam hardly carried anything but the soiled suit on his back. To avoid further friction between the two leaders, the exhausted Revere agreed to go with John Lowell to the tavern to get Hancock's trunk, *"if John would leave Lexington when they returned with it."* *"It was not until break of day,"* Dolly Quincy later revealed, *"after Mister Hancock was all night cleaning his gun and sword, that he could be persuaded that it was improper for him to expose himself against such a powerful force. . . . At that time,"* Dolly added, *"I should have been very glad to have got rid of him."*

Fat Colonel Smith with 700 Redcoats, had milled about the East Cambridge marshland until 2 a.m., awaiting needed supplies from Boston before he could march on to Lexington and Concord. Smith sent out spy John Howe in civilian clothes to ride like Revere through the countryside to alert Tories that *"The Regulars are out and marching to Concord."* He also sent Major Pitcairn and Major Mitchell ahead with a detachment of troops as an advance guard. After hearing from Revere that the countryside had been alerted, Major Mitchell returned to meet up with Colonel Smith at about 3:30 a.m. near Menotomy, and told him what Revere said. Hearing this, Smith sent Private Howe, just back from his rounds, to Boston for reinforcements. Three members of the Committee on Safety, Colonel Jeremiah Lee, Elbridge Gerry, and Ayor Orne, all Marbleheaders, who were at the meeting at Wetherby's Tavern in Menotomy with Hancock and Adams earlier that evening, were sleeping at the tavern when the British marched through the village. The three Marbleheaders quickly slipped out the back door of the tavern in their nightshirts and hid in a nearby field. Minutes later Redcoats entered the tavern, searching everywhere in the building for *"members of the Rebel Congress."* They ripped up bedding and broke down doors. Finding nothing of interest to them, they marched off to Lexington. It was almost Dawn before the three shivering men dared to return to the tavern. *"Colonel Lee was soon after attacked with a severe fever,"* wrote Elbridge Gerry, *"which resulted in his death."* Gerry, of whom John Adams once remarked, *"is opposed to everything he does not propose,"* survived the bone-chilling night in the field, and later became Vice-President of the United States.

Major Pitcairn, who had been itching for a fight with the Rebels for a long time, was chosen by Colonel Smith to lead six companies of Redcoats ahead of the main column to secure Concord's two bridges, North and South, leading in and out of that town. It was Dawn when he rode, and his men marched, onto Lexington Green. *"We saw a militia company assembled and other spectators milling about,"* the Major later reported, *"and I ordered them to lay down their arms and disperse."* Captain Parker, leader of the Minutemen, had called his men out of Buckman Tavern and onto the green, because the tavern was getting too crowded. They were assembled *"merely to consult on what to do,"* said Parker, *"and concluded not to meddle or mix with the regular troops unless they should insult or molest us."* Captain Parker told his men, some 77 in number and outnumbered ten to one, *"don't fire unless fired on, but if they mean to have war, let it begin here."*

Revere, who was now tugging on Hancock's trunk with John Lowell, on the second floor of Buckman Tavern overlooking the green, heard bells ringing and drums beating. He looked out the window and saw *"my neighbor"* Major John Pitcairn, with Major Mitchell, and a British sergeant riding *"my horse."* He and the prim and proper Mr. Lowell hurriedly struggled down the stairs with the heavy trunk, out the door, and wobbled across the green, straining with the trunk through the confused and milling ranks of Minutemen. Pitcairn halted his troops on the green, about 150 feet away as he, Major Mitchell, and the sergeant, riding *"Meg,"* rode to the front of the column of Redcoats, who had their loaded muskets with unsheathed bayonets ready for battle. *"Don't fire,"* the Major ordered his men, but as the words were out of his mouth, someone did fire his musket, but to this day no one knows who. *"A gun fired — I heard the report,"* said Revere, *"and I turned my head. . . . There was smoke, and a great shout."* Paul Revere's horse bolted and the British sergeant riding her couldn't control her. She headed in a wild gallop towards Paul, either because she spotted him, or the gunshot frightened her. *"Disperse ye Rebels, ye villains,"* shouted Pitcairn. A second shot pierced the Major's horse, wounding her, and British Lieutenant Sutherland's horse also bolted. Sutherland later swore that the first shot came from the Rebels, *"either from behind a nearby stonewall, or from a window at Buckman Tavern."* Captain Parker ordered his men to withdraw as the Redcoats broke rank and began chasing some of the Minutemen. At this moment, Colonel Smith with the main body of Redcoats arrived on the scene. Everyone was firing in different directions. Even fat Aunt Lydia Hancock, who was leaning out a window at Clark's Parsonage to see what was going on, had a bullet crease her ear. Minuteman Jon Harrington, who lived by the Green, was shot in the chest, and crawled to his house to die on his front steps at his wife's feet. Another Minuteman was wounded, then stabbed by a Redcoat as he knelt in prayer. In what the British commanders considered *"a quick skirmish,"* eight Americans were killed and ten were wounded. Major Pitcairn quickly reorganized his troops, and after three loud *"huzzas"* on the Green *"for victory,"* the Redcoats marched off towards Concord.

About this time, Revere and Lowell arrived at Clark's Parsonage with the trunk. *"King"* Hancock and *"Citizen"* Adams, as Dolly Quincy jokingly nicknamed them, were sitting impatiently in a carriage outside. The trunk was hoisted onto the carriage. They then headed off down Bedford Road, away from the British, towards Burlington and another *"safe-house"* parsonage. The sounds of gunfire still buzzing in his ears, Sam Adams shouted into the sky, *"Oh, what a glorious morning this is!" "Yes, it is a nice day,"* replied Hancock — John thought Sam was talking about the weather.

By the time Major John Pitcairn's detachment, still marching ahead of Colonel Smith's main body of Redcoats, arrived at Concord, about 7:30 a.m., the Concord Minutemen had hidden most of their munitions or had carted supplies away to other towns. Cannons had been ploughed under by farmers in their fields, musketballs had been stuffed into feather mattresses, cannonballs had been dropped into the shallows of the river, and much of the gunpowder was hidden in the court-house. Pitcairn first decided to make Wright Tavern his temporary headquarters in town, but proprietor Ephraim Jones locked the tavern door and wouldn't let him in. The Major put his shoulder to the door and, with the help of some of his men, broke it in. As Pitcairn entered, Jones wrestled him to the floor and socked him in the jaw. The Major put a pistol to Jones' head and threatened to kill him. *"We know you are hiding cannons here,"* said the Major, *"and if you don't bring us to them, I will fire."* Jones reluctantly escorted Pitcairn to the nearby jail-yard, where three 24-pounder cannons stood on wooden carriages, the only cannons the Minutemen hadn't had time to hide. The Redcoats knocked off the cannon trunions, and then burned the carriages, which caused little damage to the cannons — they were later repaired and used by the Minutemen. While the soldiers amused themselves with the bonfire, Pitcairn ordered Jones to make breakfast and pour *"wake-me-*

up" drinks for him and his officers back at the tavern. As the Major sat stirring his brandy with his finger, he shouted to Jones who was making breakfast, *"I hope to stir damned Yankee blood before nightfall."*

Colonel Smith's troops arrived after ransacking a few farmhouses along the way, and they stood in the road, weary and hungry after their all night march. A squad of them, after searching the court-house and finding nothing of military value, put the building to the torch, but 80-year old Mrs. Moulton who lived next door to the court-house, insisted that the Redcoats put out the fire. They obeyed her, which was lucky for them all, for the gunpowder hidden in the court-house could have blown everyone skyhigh. Colonel Smith, weary himself, allowed his troops to rest and have a bite to eat from their kits, but British spy John Howe had told him that a Colonel Barrett, who lived two miles out of town near the North Bridge, had munitions stored at his home. Smith sent out a detachment of six companies under Captains Laurie and Parsons to search Barrett's house and farm and to destroy the bridge.

As church bells rang from village to village and town to town, all the way to New Hampshire and Connecticut, drummerboys hastened to the village Greens and town commons to gather the militiamen and Minutemen to march to Concord. At neighboring Bedford, Captain Jon Wilson met his men at Fitch's Tavern. *"It's a cold breakfast,"* he said to them, *"but we'll give the British a hot dinner."* They marched off — Wilson was dead before dinner. At the nearby village of Acton, Captain Issac Davis, normally a quiet man, shouted at Minutemen Abner Hosman and Jim Hayward, who kept horsing around and joking, as their small band tromped through the woods to Concord — none of them would see another day. They joined some other Minutemen from Lincoln and Concord on the high hill overlooking Concord's North Bridge at about 8:30 a.m. It was turning out to be a warm April day — in more ways than one. They saw the British detachment under Captain Laurie march to the bridge and halt, as another under Captain Parsons crossed the bridge and marched off to Barrett's farm, where the illegal munitions stored there had been hidden under a bed of flowers. Some 400 Minutemen now gathered on the hill, outnumbering Captain Laurie's Redcoats at the bridge below, but since they had no knowledge of what had happened at Lexington, some were opposed to firing on the British. The Concord men spotted the smoke rising from town, either from the court-house or from the burning cannon carriages. *"Will you let them burn down our town?"* shouted Minuteman Major John Buttrick. *"I haven't a man that's afraid to go,"* spoke up Captain Issac Davis, and the Acton Minutemen started down the hill toward the bridge with the others following.

Seeing the Minutemen approach, Captain Laurie's Redcoats tried to quickly take up the bridge plankings. Major Buttrick shouted across the bridge for them to stop. The British fired a few warning shots across the narrow Concord river. Buttrick turned to his Minutemen and shouted, *"Fire, men, for God's sake, fire!"* Three Redcoats dropped dead and nine others were wounded in this first volley from the Minutemen. Longfellow memoralized this moment with: *"By the rude bridge that arched the flood — Their flag to April's breeze unfurled — Here once the embattled farmers stood — And fired the shot heard round the world."*

The British then fired and Issac Davis dropped dead. The Americans reloaded and started to cross the bridge. The Redcoats broke ranks. Four of their officers were wounded, including Captain Laurie and Lieutenant Sutherland — they retreated. From a house overlooking the bridge, called *"The Old Manse, "* Reverend William Emerson watched the battle. One of Emerson's *"half-witted"* farm hands rushed from the Manse and pounced on a wounded Redcoat whom the others had left behind by the bridge, and chopped him to death with an axe. Hearing the gun-fire, Colonel Smith reorganized his troops and started marching towards the bridge, leaving his horse behind, but he was so fat he couldn't walk very fast. His retreating detachment met him less than a quarter-mile out of town. Smith then waited for Parsons' detachment to return from their unsuccessful search at Barrett's farm. The Colonel returned to town, marching the Redcoats up and down the main street, waiting for his reinforcements from Boston. Minutemen gathered nearby, the American drums and fifes beating and blaring, and unnerving Colonel Smith. The Colonel had his fifers play *"Yankee Doodle"* in an attempt to drown out the American music, but Colonel Smith was tired and anxious. He couldn't understand what had happened to the reinforcements that he had called for some six hours earlier. He decided to march his troops back to Lexington, and on the way out of Concord, a Redcoat took a shot at the mingling Minutemen, which was a mistake, for that parting shot infuriated the confused Minutemen and rallied them. They pursued the Redcoats to Lexington, ducking behind walls, fences, and trees, taking shots at the trailing columns. By the time the British reached Lexington Green again, some twenty to thirty Redcoats had been wounded by Concord's Minutemen snipers. The Colonel allowed his men to rest for a moment at Lexington, and then they started on their long twenty mile march back to Boston, Minutemen taking pot-shots at them all along the way. Colonel Smith would have been willing to surrender, but there was no one to surrender to —

just a puff of smoke from behind a bush or tree, and another Redcoat would fall — this wasn't battle as the British knew it — the Americans were fighting like *"sneaky Indians."*

Colonel Smith's 700-man army was saved when, some two miles out of Lexington, the long awaited British reinforcements arrived, some 900 Redcoats under Major General Percy, Dolly Quincy's old boyfriend who had, a few days earlier, called New Englanders *"timid cowards."* His delay in coming was caused by a one hour holdup in Boston looking for Major Pitcairn, who (Percy hadn't realized) had gone off earlier with Colonel Smith. He had been further delayed two hours by little George Hewes and some of the Liberty Boys of Boston, who had destroyed the Cambridge bridge, making it impossible for the troops to pass on to Cambridge until it was repaired. Percy took command on their march back to Boston, his troops taking up the rear to protect Colonel Smith's rear columns that were slowly being shot away.

Doc Warren left Boston about the same time Percy and his reinforcements did. He took a boat to Cambridge, then borrowed a carriage and rode to Menotomy (Arlington) where many Minutemen from outlying towns and villages were congregating. He, with the help of *"Fatty"* Bill Heath of Roxbury, organized the various groups and prepared them for an all-out assault on the British as they passed through the town. It was here in Menotomy that the Redcoats were caught in a heavy crossfire from houses and taverns that flanked the road. Many Redcoats broke ranks and chased Minutemen into these houses and taverns. At Jason Russel's home in Menotomy, not only was Russel himself killed, but 11 other Minutemen were shot and bayoneted by Redcoats. By the time the weary and demoralized British troops reached Cambridge Bridge, which Hewes and the Liberty Boys of Boston and Cambridge had wrecked again, making it impassable, they had suffered 273 casualties. Colonel Smith was wounded, Major Pitcairn had his horse shot from under him — permanently this time — and 106 Redcoats had been killed or captured by the Minutemen. Of the Minutemen, militiamen, and a few innocent civilians, 49 were killed and another 40 wounded. Doctor Ben Church, who had been at Menotomy, had blood in his shoes, covering his face and his clothes, which he said *"was splattered on me by a militia man battling beside me,"* and Doc Warren had part of his hair shot away by a musket-ball.

As the sun set, Percy marched his troops to Bunker Hill, Charlestown, as some 3,000 of the pursuing Minutemen met on Charlestown Common. Percy contacted General Gage in Boston, suggesting that the troops remain camped on the highground of Charlestown, but Gage sent over rowboats from Boston, that night, and ordered the army to return to Boston. Doc Warren had the Minutemen reassemble on Cambridge Common. *"The country militia, like a moving circle, surrounded and followed us wherever we went,"* Lord Percy explained to General Gage the next morning. *"The Rebels attacked in a very scattered, irregular manner, but with perseverence and resolution.... For fifteen miles they followed and pelted us, we scarce had time to draw a trigger.... Whoever looks upon them as an irregular mob, will find himself mistaken. They have men about them who know very well what they are about."* Percy no longer considered them *"timid cowards."*

"Bloody Butchery of British Troops" headlined the newspapers next day, and the written stories of the battles from the American point of view were immediately shipped off to England by Warren's sea-messenger John Derby of Salem, before Gage's watered-down version of what happened could reach the British people. Warren also quickly distributed copies of his *"Address to the Inhabitants of Great Britain and America's Provincial Congress."* In this address, Warren said, *"to give a particular account of the ravages of the troops as they retreated from Concord to Charlestown would be very difficult. Let it suffice to say that a great number of the houses on the road were plundered and rendered unfit for use, several were burned, women in childbed were driven by the soldiery naked into the streets, old men peaceably in their houses were shot dead, and such scenes exhibited as would disgrace the annals of the most uncivilized nation.... To the persecution and tyranny of the King's cruel Ministry, we will not tamely submit — appealing to Heaven for the justice of our cause, we determine to die or be free."* As John Adams so aptly put it, *"The long years of Revolution ended at Lexington and Concord, and the war began."*

King George III, who eventually went insane, and Sam Adams, who helped to stimulate the King's insanity — this statue of Sam stands defiantly in front of Faneuil Hall, Boston. The hall was the major meeting house for the Rebels. An engraving of The Battle at Bunker's Hill, the death of Doctor Joe Warren and of British Major Pitcairn, courtesy of the Essex Institute, Salem, MA.

VI
AN APPEAL TO HEAVEN

As John Hancock and Sam Adams meandered their merry way to Philadelphia to meet with John Adams and the Colonial Congress, Paul Revere and Joe Warren were being kept extremely busy. The versatile Revere was not only scurrying here and there delivering messages, but was also ordered by Congress to engrave and print colonial currency and *"soldier's notes"* at Watertown, Massachusetts, in order to pay the Minutemen and Militia Companies with whom Warren pleaded to remain in Cambridge to keep the British besieged in Boston. Revere made the paper money so thick that it got the name *"pasteboard currency."* Revere was also called to Philadelphia to learn how to make gunpowder, and was then asked to manufacture the precious powder at an old mill in Canton, Massachusetts. *"Your orders are to proceed to Titicut,"* came an added demand from the Provincial Congress, *"to make enquiry how they go on in the casting of brass and iron cannons. . . ."* Warren, who was deemed unofficial Commander-in-Chief of the armed forces in Cambridge, needed weapons, especially cannons and gunpowder desperately, so he kept his trusty lieutenant Paul Revere in the thick of things. When Paul couldn't procure certain ammunition, weapons or equipment, he was ordered to make the items himself — thus Paul got involved in the making of money, gunpowder, cannons, and other iron, copper, and brass items necessary for the war effort. He even had women melting down pewter pots, mugs and dishes, and lead window-weights, molding them into musket-balls. For the ragamuffin American volunteers who either forgot to bring their fowling-pieces and muskets to Cambridge, or didn't own a weapon, Warren had Revere's mechanics make them pikes and hand-spears, hoping they might prove a worthy defense against British bayonets.

"There never were such tatter-demalions," said General Gage from Boston. *"They are a rustic-rout with calico-frocks and foul pieces, unkempt and undisciplined,"* he assured his troops. He couldn't wait to meet them in a face-to-face *"honorable battle"* with his 13,600 polished and highly disciplined regulars. Warren, in fact, feared Gage would attack at any moment, but the General and his Redcoats were temporarily locked into Boston, running low on food and other necessities of life, unable to acquire them unless shipped from Halifax, Nova Scotia or from Mother England. Gage wrote to the King's Ministry for supplies and for more troops to *"crush this rebellion."* An added worry for Gage were all the anti-British Whigs and Sons of Liberty in town. He decided to allow anyone who wished to leave Boston to do so, but

they would have to leave all their possessions behind, and check all their weapons with the British guards on the way out. The General collected 1,778 muskets and 634 pistols, as some 14,000 anti-British residents left Boston. The only ones whom Gage forbade to leave were *"cooks, carpenters, and fishermen,"* and the families of such *"traitors"* as Paul Revere and Joseph Warren. George Hewes was considered a fisherman, so the British wouldn't let him go. He was forced to fish from a rowboat in Boston Bay every day, under guard, to help feed the British soldiers. Some of his fishermen friends dove into the water, and amidst musket fire, swam to where the Americans had set up crude defenses along the shore facing Boston. George, however, never learned to swim, and had almost drowned trying to learn when he was a boy.

One day, General Gage sent a note by messenger to Warren, offering to *"pardon all, but Sam Adams and John Hancock, if you all will lay down your arms."* Warren replied with a note that read: *"I will pardon all who will surrender to our Army, except Thomas Gage."* Warren also sent out a personal plea to the Committees of Safety in every New England village and town. *"An Army is needed,"* he wrote, *"to defend our wives and children. We beg and entreat you to save our country from absolute slavery."* The Massachusetts Provincial Congress called for 8,000 men, over and above the militia, to serve seven months. Some 2,000 Connecticut men under the fearless rolly-polly tavern-keeper, 59 year old Isreal Putnam rolled into Cambridge with four cannons, and Nat Greene arrived with two cannons and 1,500 Rhode Islanders. Other New Englanders were jealous of the Rhode Island boys, for they had brought along real tents to sleep in, whereas others camped in and around Cambridge Common were forced to use old torn sails to sleep under. Even Benedict Arnold came up from Connecticut and convinced Warren that with 400 men he could get needed cannons and ammunition from the British held Fort Ticonderoga on Lake Champlain. Warren agreed to give it a try, but Arnold had to do his own recruiting outside Cambridge. On May 15, Arnold, with Ethan Allen and his Green Mountain Boys, took the fort without a casualty on either side, and 300-pound Henry Knox was sent to upstate New York with a group of teamsters, given the almost impossible mission to bring the 58 captured cannons and mortars from the fort back to Cambridge.

On the hot morning of June 7th, Joe Warren, fatigued and feeling sick, started a long walk towards Charlestown. Elbridge Gerry tried to stop him, but Warren insisted that he be there at Breed's Hill where, the night before, Colonel William Prescott with some 400 men had built a

100-yard square and five-feet deep redoubt fortification. It was on a narrow peninsula below Bunker Hill, overlooking the Mystic River on one side and the Charles River on the other, facing Boston. General Gage watched *"Old Put"* and his Connecticut boys arrive and take up positions on the hill that morning. Massachusetts' and Rhode Island's rag-tag armies dug in at the redoubt. Late arrivals were the New Hampshire men under John Sullivan and John Stark. They had traveled 62 miles with oxcarts filled with the gunpowder Sullivan and his men had confiscated and hidden after their earlier attack on Fort William And Mary. Putnam said he was at the moment, *"Praying for gunpowder."* He turned around *"and there it was."* The flag flying next to Putnam in the redoubt carried the motto, *"An Appeal To Heaven."* So here they were, *"the rustic-rout in calico frocks,"* ready for a *"face-to-face"* confrontation with Gage's regulars but, because of an oversight on Gage's part, the rustics now controlled the high ground. Gage had no choice but to attack.

Six British warships and six British batteries at Copp's Hill, Boston, 168 cannons in all, started firing at Breed's Hill early in the morning, and hot cannon-balls dropping on nearby Charlestown, completely destroyed every home and building in the town. British troops, however, weren't ferried across the river in barges to the Charlestown side until 1:30 p.m., about the same time Doc Warren showed up at the redoubt. Prescott offered to turn over command of the American troops to Warren, but he refused, saying he would fight as a regular foot soldier this day. Six regiments of Redcoats under General William Howe attacked the hill at 3 p.m.; when 40 yards from the American front line, they were forced to retreat, some 96 of their number lying dead or wounded in the grass. They tried again, 600 Redcoats this time, straight up the hill, but again they were repulsed by the stinging fire of what Gage had called *"old fowling pieces."* Putnam had told his men not to fire *"'til you see the whites of their eyes,"* and John Stark had set a stick in the ground 40 yards from his barricade, telling his men not to fire *"'Til the Redcoats pass that stick."* The men obeyed their commanders and it wasn't hard for them to miss the long human lines of scarlet coats advancing on them at that close range. The Americans, however, were running out of ammunition. Howe, crying with frustrated rage, sent a messenger to General Gage in Boston that he needed more troops. Some of Howe's companies had no more than two or three soldiers left in them.

Once Howe had his reinforcements, the final charge up Breed's Hill was a due or die attempt for the British. As one Minuteman said, *"We had repulsed them many times and, after bearing for about two hours, many fired away their ammunition."* Said a British soldier, *"none of the Americans had bayonets, nothing but fists, clubbed muskets and rocks, but they fought on, more like Devils than men."* Salem Prince, a freed slave, with his last round of ammunition, shot Major Pitcairn in the chest and killed him. Redcoats poured into Prescott's redoubt where there was bloody hand-to-hand combat. As Joe Warren tried to escape from the redoubt, he was shot in the head by a British marine and he dropped to the blood-soaked earth, dead. The British pursued the retreating Americans to Bunker Hill, some 200 yards behind Breed's Hill, where Putnam made a last-ditch defense so that many Americans could escape over the Charlestown causeway to Cambridge. Then Old Put and his men made good their escape. The British now held the high ground, but they had paid too dearly for it. Although the Americans lost 115 men, with 355 wounded and 30 captured, the British lost 226 regulars, with 828 wounded, one-fourth of their attacking army, and 145 of their casualties were high ranking officers. The great British Empire had never suffered such a defeat on the battleground. General Gage was so surprised at the outcome that he was heard to say, *"These Rebels are not the despicable rabble too many of us have supposed."* The King's Ministry soon ordered Gage back to England, *"a broken man,"* said one of his officers, and General William Howe took command of the British troops in Boston.

Of Warren, a British officer commented, *"He was stuffed with another Rebel into a hole, and there he and his seditious principles will remain."* Said John Adams' wife Abigail, *"Not all the havoc and devastation they have made, has wounded me like the death of Warren."* Like Abigail, most Americans were devastated at hearing of Warren's death. *"Warren was one of the shining lights of the Colonies,"* said Paul Revere, *"and the first great martyr to the national cause."*

Seven days after *"The Battle of Bunker Hill,"* the new Congress meeting at Philadelphia, with John Hancock as their chosen President, asked for the mustering of sharp-shooting riflemen from Maryland, Pennsylvania, and Virginia, *"to assist New England."* Over 1,400 riflemen volunteered and began their long trek to Cambridge, Massachusetts. It was John Adams who convinced Congress that George Washington of Virginia would be the ideal Commander-In-Chief for the American Army, and the new General also headed out, on horseback, to Cambridge. He arrived 15 days after the battle. Washington's first impression of the New England troops was *"They are an exceedingly dirty and nasty people. There is an unaccountable kind of stupidity in the lower class of these New Englanders,"* he told Richard Henry Lee, his second in command, *"which, believe me, prevails too generally among the officers of the Massachusetts part of the Army.... The men regard their officers as no more than broomsticks."*

When the Virginia riflemen arrived, they almost immediately clashed with the Massachusetts men, especially the Marblehead *"Amphibious Regiment"* under Colonel John Glover, Paul Revere's cousin by marriage. One day, 1,000 officers and men from Virginia and Marblehead got into a brawl, and the 6-foot 2-inch General Washington, on horseback, charged the lot of them and, without a word, grabbed two brawlers by their throats and lifted them off the ground, shaking them like rag-dolls. *"From the moment I saw Washington leap the bars at Cambridge and realized his personal ascendancy over the turbulent tempers of his men in their moments of wildest excitement,"* said New Hampshire's John Sullivan, *"I never faltered in the faith that we had the right man to lead the cause of American liberty."* Washington brought discipline to the camp at Cambridge, even to the point of personal hygiene and table manners — *"Feed not with greediness,"* was one of his orders, apparently aimed at the Massachusetts men. *"Cut your bread with your knife, lean not on the table, neither find fault with what you eat."* He passed out ribbons and cockades of different colors for the officers to wear, so that the lower ranking men could distinguish them — the Majors wore pink. Washington ordered *"When your superiors talk, hear them, but neither speak nor laugh."* Washington also outlawed the celebration of Guy Fawkes Day on November 5th, which he said, *"is so monstrous, it is not to be suffered or excused. It is a ridiculous and childish custom."* Washington was a take-charge guy, and John Adams couldn't have made a better choice.

The only member of Sam Adams' old secret society of freedom fighters that remained at American Army Headquarters at Cambridge, was Doctor Ben Church. The *"beloved Church,"* as Sam and the others called him, ran the Army Hospital. Once, he was even allowed to sneak into Boston on a spying mission for the Commander-In-Chief. It was Nat Greene, the Commander of the Rhode Island troops, who received a letter from friends in Newport, confiscated from a female spy who was trying to slip it to a British officer, that changed everyone's mind about Church. The letter contained information on American troops, supplies, and fortifications at Cambridge. The female spy was Benjamin Church's pregnant mistress. After hours of interrogation by Washington's men, she admitted that Church had written the treasonous letter. It was also soon discovered that Church hadn't been active in the battle of Menotomy as he declared, but had splattered pig's blood all over himself to make others think he was a hero. He was the British spy whom Paul Revere and Joe Warren feared was in their midst from the beginning of the Liberty Party movement, but neither patriot would ever think of distrusting Ben Church. Washington had him arrested and thrown in jail, where he remained for five years. Convicted of treason, he was banished from America in 1780. While sailing to England, his ship was lost in a storm, and neither the Americans nor the British ever heard from their *"beloved Ben Church"* again.

With all this heavy intrigue going on in the Cambridge camp, the heavy Henry Knox was dragging 58 cannons and mortars, some of them weighing 5,000 pounds apiece, 300 miles from upstate New York and over the snowy Berkshire Mountains, using 80 yoke of oxen. He arrived in Cambridge camp in late February, 1776. Though exhausted, Washington made Henry climb one more hill with his cannons, to the top of Dorchester Heights. By March 2nd, the cannons began blasting the 78 British warships that were anchored in Boston Harbor, and by March 14th, 2,000 Americans had completely fortified Dorchester Heights overlooking Boston. General Howe sent Lord Percy with 3,000 Redcoats to attack the Heights, but a wild storm stopped them from even landing in Dorchester — another *"appeal to heaven, by Old Put,"* was the rumor in camp — *"Putnam's prayers brought on the storm."* At about this same time, another minor miracle occurred, a rowboat with a solitary little figure in it, his hands almost frozen to the oars, landed at Lynn Beach, some 13 miles north of Boston. George Hewes had made good his escape. While fishing for the British in Boston Harbor, when the roar of the cannons from Dorchester Heights surprised and distracted his guards who were in another boat, George started rowing as hard as he could out of the Harbor and through the night to Lynn.

"That evening I had dinner with George Washington at Cambridge," reported Hewes, *"and he laughed at my escape. . . . He didn't really laugh,"* Hewes corrected himself, *"but he looked amazingly good natured. . . . Madame Washington waited on us and was remarkably social."* George Hewes informed the General on the British defenses, and told him that the Tories and 13,000 British troops were becoming demoralized in Boston because of lack of food and slow shipments from Halifax, *"their food cargo vessels often being captured by privateersmen."* Washington was obviously captivated by this midget Minuteman, and Hewes asked the General if he might join the new American Army. The General said he would be honored to have George Hewes serve under him — his size was no longer a detriment to enlistment.

George Hewes, with George Washington, to the tune of *"Yankee*

Doodle" marched triumphantly into Boston on March 20th, three days after General Howe and his troops, with 1,000 Tories, *"quitted the town"* and sailed for Halifax. The reason for the British departure was that Washington now knew all the locations of Howe's troops and defenses, thanks to Hewes, and he informed Howe that he planned to destroy all Boston fortifications from Dorchester Heights. Washington also told General Howe he preferred that the British evacuate than to have Boston destroyed. General Howe complied but, before leaving, the British soldiers demolished almost every church in Boston and cut down the Liberty Tree. Otherwise, the town was intact. George Hewes was pleased to hear that when the Liberty Tree fell, a limb of it landed on a British soldier, crushing him to death. Where the tree once stood, George Washington addressed his six month old Army. The British, in their haste to get out of Boston, had left behind gunpowder, ammunition and 250 cannons — which brought a rousing cheer from the Americans who were just about out of ammunition. New England was free, but the American Army must now march on to free all of America from British rule. *"With our faith,"* said Washington, *"lays the destiny of unborn millions.'*

On August 13, 1835, over 60 years after Boston's celebrated *"Evacuation Day,"* a small article appeared in the Boston newspaper. It read: *"A ninety-six years old man, said to be the last surviving member of the Boston Tea Party, visited Boston this week from his residence in New York. His name is George Robert Twelves Hewes."* George served with distinction, active in many battles, throughout the Revolutionary War. One wonders in retrospect, would we have our precious liberty today if it weren't for the efforts, be it sometimes accidental, of this mischievous little Minuteman.

Statue of George Washington on horesback, stands in Boston Garden in the downtown area, overlooking Boston Common near the site of the Liberty Tree.

New England's
RIOTOUS REVOLUTION

BIBLIOGRAPHY

Bosson, Albert, *The Battle of Chelsea.* Old Suffolk Chapter, Sons of the American Revolution, Register (1900)

Bowen, Catherine Drinker, *John Adams and the American Revolution.* Little, Brown & Co., Boston, 1950.

Brown, Abram English, *John Hancock, His Book.* Lee & Shepard Publishers, Boston, 1898.

Cary, John, *Joseph Warren — Physician, Politician, Patriot.* University of Illinois Press, Urbana, 1961.

Coffin, C.C., *The Boys of '76.* Harper & Brothers, New York, 1924.

Drake, Samuel Adams, *Historic Mansions and Highways Around Boston.* Little, Brown & Co., Boston, 1873.

Early, Eleanor, *New England Sampler.* Waverly House, Boston, MA, 1940.

Field, Edward, *The Colonial Tavern.* Preston & Rounds, Providence, RI, 1897.

Fiore, Jordan D., *Massachusetts in Ferment.* Bicentennial Commission, Publishers, Boston, 1971.

Fox, Ebenezer, *The Revolutionary Adventures.* Monroe & Francis, Publishers, Boston, 1838.

French, Allen, *The Day at Concord and Lexington.* Little, Brown & Co., Boston, 1925.

Gay Transcripts: State Papers, XII 40-97 depositions (Aug. 25, 1770 dated).

Greene, R.E., *Black Defenders of America.* Johnson Publishing Co., Inc., Chicago, 1974.

Griffin, Bulkley S., *Offbeat History.* World Publishing Co., Cleveland, Ohio, 1967.

Hayward, W.S., *Paul Revere and the American Revolution.* Thesis, PhD. Harvard University, 1933.

Holbrook, Stewart, *The Yankee Exodus.* The MacMillan Co., New York, 1950.

Howe, Octavias T., *Massachusetts on the Seas in the War of the Revolution.* (1775-1783), Mass. Prov. Cong. Journals, pp. 291-308, Hart, ed. Commonwealth History III, 31.

Klingberg, F.J., *The Morning of America.* D. Appleton-Century Co., New York, 1941.

Knollenberg, B., *Washington and the Revolution.* The MacMillan Co., New York, 1940.

Lecky, W.E.H., *The American Revolution.* D. Appleton and Co., New York, 1921.

Lodge, H.C., *The Story of the Revolution.* C. Scribner's Sons, New York, 1898.

Longley, Ronald S., *Mobs in Revolutionary Massachusetts.* New England Quarterly, Vol. VI No.1, (March 1933).

Martin, Joseph Plumb, *Private Yankee Doodle.* Edited by George F. Scheer, Popular Library, Publishers, New York, 1963.

McIlwain, C.H., *The American Revolution.* The MacMillan Co., New York, 1924.

Miller, Nathan, *Sea of Glory.* David McKay Co. Inc., New York, 1974.

Neumann, George C., *The History of Weapons of the American Revolution.* Harper & Row, New York, 1967.

Revolutionary War Bicentennial Commission & Trustees of the Boston Public Library, *Blood in the Streets — The Boston Massacre.* Boston, 1970.

Thatcher, Benjamin B., *Traits of the Tea Party — Memoir of George T. Hewes.* Harper & Brothers, Publisher, New York, 1835.

Thatcher, Benjamin B., *George Robert Twelves Hewes — Memoirs.* 1937.

Van Doren, C., *Secret History of the American Revolution.* The Viking Press, New York, 1941.

Van Tyne, C.H., *The War of Independence.* Houghton-Mifflin Co., Boston, 1829.

Wroth, L. Kinvin and Hiller B. Zobel (edited by), *The Legal Papers of John Adams.* Belknap Press, 1965.